S T A T E S

Scale of Miles
0   100   200

NUEVO
LEÓN

Monterrey

GULF

OF

MEXICO

Norte

TAMAULIPAS

N LUIS   Tula
POTOSÍ

Luis Potosí   R. Panuco   Tampico

JUATO   Dolores
Hidalgo   ORO.
Guanajuato   HIDALGO
Querétaro

MÉXICO
México   TLAX.
ACÁN   D.F.   Puebla
Cuernavaca   MOR.   Fortín
R.   PUEBLA
Balsas   Tehuácán

GUERRERO   OAXACA
MITLA

Acapulco

VERA
CRUZ   Veracruz

R.
Coatzacoalcos   TABASCO

R.

CHIAPAS
R.
Grijalva   Usumacinta

Mérida
YUCATÁN

Campeche

CAMPECHE

QUINTANA ROO

BR.
HONDURAS

GUATEMALA

AN

D1737211

Discarded
7/25/05

HERE IS MEXICO

Distances
cyclical

HERE IS MEXICO

Elizabeth Borton de Treviño

FARRAR, STRAUS & GIROUX
NEW YORK

An Ariel Book

To Jenny B. Gerber,
passionate devotee of Mexico
for more than fifty years,
I dedicate this book

Author's Apology

I quite understand that there are many readers who would like a kind of orientation on Mexico; an idea of the taste, smell, feeling, and rhythm of Mexico; and perhaps a few basic ideas about Mexico's history, sociology, and geography. For these readers, it is obvious that a short and necessarily superficial book could provide many answers.

Yet, when I began to plan how to write this book, it became increasingly apparent to me that my account would not only skim over countless fascinating facets of what constitutes Mexico, but would have to be, because of its length and purpose, an extremely personal view.

In choosing facts and impressions which mean Mexico and which illuminate one or another of the qualities of this country and its people, I have simply written about the things that interest me. No doubt many important ideas and facts and analyses are left out, and for these and for my errors, whether of fact or of interpretation, I ask pardon. My excuse is that the writer is a person who truly loves Mexico.

Elizabeth Borton de Treviño

HERE IS MEXICO

1

Mexico.

What is Mexico?

A place. A country. A people. A way of life. A great history. A fascinating art.

Many things.

There are many Mexicos.

The Mexico of the indigenous peoples. The Mexico of the ruins, the pyramids, the ancient, deserted cities. The Mexico of the great cathedrals and monasteries built like fortresses. The Mexico of Juárez. The Mexico of the world's first great land revolution, predating the Russian Revolution by almost ten years. The Mexico of the fiery muralists. The Mexico of today.

However, despite Mexico's astounding variety, there are

things that Mexico is *not,* and before attempting to get a picture and a taste of Mexico, one should be aware of the erroneous attitudes and impressions that should be set aside regarding this spectacular country.

Mexico is *not* a little Spain.

While it is true that Spanish is the official language of Mexico, and Spanish traditions and culture have acted upon and influenced Mexican social structure and thought —and Mexicans and Spaniards share a passion for the bull-fight—Mexico is not a reflection of Spain. Mexicans dislike being called "Spaniards" by thoughtless people; on the contrary, they are intensely proud of being Mexican. A clue to Mexican feeling about Spain and Spain's years of holding Mexico as a colony is the fact that in the capital there is not one street named Cortes, nor one public statue in his honor. He was the conqueror. And though he and Christian friars gave Mexico the Christian faith—still professed today by 95 percent of the people—which supplanted the terrible human sacrifices that characterized the Indian religion, and though he brought the language and the law that (with certain modifications) are in use today, and though he gave Mexico the first university in the Americas, and the first free public hospital, he was never loved, but always sullenly resented. And that is true to a great degree even today.

Cortes loved Mexico and stipulated in his will that his body was to be buried in the land he had taken and brought under the rule of Spain. And yet today nobody knows for certain where his bones lie.

Still another point. While Mexico is not a little Spain, neither is it an "Indian country," nor are the picturesque remnants of the original Indian peoples the most active or the most powerful or the most influential group in the Republic. They are not even the most numerous, constituting only 10 percent of the population.

Mexicans are a fusion of the aboriginal tribes (and there were many of these, quite different one from the other) and the Spaniard. The result is a new people, strong, aggressive, and as determined as the Spaniard, yet as subtle, poetic, gentle, and taciturn as the Indian.

In the matter of geography, Mexico is neither a desert country nor a mountain country nor a tropical country, but all three. The north is dry and sun-baked and rain-parched; the central plateaus are high (almost all the important cities are located 6,000 feet or more above sea level) and temperate, whereas the southern section is tropical. There are miles of coastline, broken by some of the most beautiful bays and beaches in the world. And like a backbone, supporting the entire Republic, are chains of mountains, the highest peaks eternally snow-covered, the sides fragrant with pine and cedar.

Mexico is not a "backward" country. She has problems that she is making every effort to solve, and these problems are interrelated and in fact inseparable. Yet steady progress can be observed, and enormous strides are being made toward the general betterment of conditions for all the people. The greatest portion of the Mexican national budget is set aside for education. (This is not the case in many reputedly progressive countries.)

Mexico is not backward in the idealistic sense either. She has elaborated a foreign policy based firmly on peace and has headed all movements to outlaw atomic power for any

5

but peaceful uses. Mexico has never attempted to conquer one inch of foreign territory, nor has she ever swerved from her conviction, upheld in her diplomacy, that the people of every country have the right of self-determination and must not be subjected to pressure or control from outside—however strongly other countries may feel that they know best what should be done and how it should be done.

Mexico has been a free and independent republic for one hundred and fifty years. Many times during those years she has had to fight and shed blood to wrench off tyrannies from outside and return to her ideal of democracy.

Mexico has lost territory totaling about one million square miles—more than her present area—to the United States; yet her southern border with the United States is not fortified. There is free movement of citizens from one country to the other, and Mexico maintains a position of honorable friendship with the stronger neighbor to the north.

How did these people, these Mexicans, come into being? Who were their ancestors?

No one is certain where the first inhabitants of Mexico came from. Scholars study and propose theories; yet others disagree. In the faces and figures and in the art of some of Mexico's people there are obvious relationships with the Orient. There may have been some connection with the tribes of the South Seas. In Yucatán and on the Caribbean coast, legends and many curious facts seem to indicate a communication, in remote times, with Europe, possibly by way of the mysterious island of Atlantis, whose sinking into the Atlantic is thought to have been the origin of all the legends of the Great Flood that appear in the folklore of so many peoples.

The facts, insofar as they can be proved, are that in the twelfth century a warlike, nomadic people called the Aztecs wandered into the Valley of Mexico and beheld a curious sight that to them seemed to have a religious significance. A great eagle, with a writhing serpent in its beak, flew down from the sky and perched upon a cactus. This sign was taken as a command from the gods for the Aztecs to cease their wanderings and make their home on that spot. (The eagle and the serpent figure today in the Mexican flag.)

The valley was richly wooded, well watered, and cradled a great central lake. The Aztecs made it their kingdom, building on and around the lake a city they called Tenochtitlán. They erected their own pyramids over others they found there, sacrificed to their own families of gods, and warred continuously against other tribes to the north and south of them.

But the Aztecs were latecomers to the country that is now Mexico. Centuries before—as early as 10,000 B.C., say some authorities (others put it earlier still)—there was a flourishing civilization of great sophistication and learning which centered around the ruins of the city now called Monte Albán, in the valley of Oaxaca. These people had observatories and marked the orbits of the stars and planets; they had discovered the concept of zero (long before Europeans did); they had a written language and a developed art. Their influence spread to the south and to the north, and it is they, scholars tell us, who devised what is known as the Aztec calendar, which was far more accurate than the calendar we use today. These mysterious people disappeared into the mists of history, as did the Mayans, who it is believed came after them and who built their own civilization to the south.

Where the Mayans came from, no one knows. Nor do we know what became of them. Some of their descendants survive in southeast Mexico and in Guatemala and Honduras; they remember little of their origins, though they retain rich memories of legend, art, poetry, and music. So indeed do the Mixtec and Zapotec peoples, who survive in the country in and around the state of Oaxaca.

Throughout the land known as Mayan country, there are mysterious ruins, vestiges of great stone cities, with houses, temples, civic centers, astronomical observatories, and squares used for religious dancing and ritual ball games. One can make out miles and miles of straight, stone-paved *sac bes*, or causeways, by means of which the Mayan cities communicated with each other. There are remains of underground water systems, and carvings on monumental stones and on temples show that the Mayans were advanced in astronomy and in arithmetic.

What must have been a great and flowering civilization, however, disappeared seemingly overnight. When the Spaniards first made landfalls in what is now Yucatán, the Mayan cities were ruins and the Indians who remained in the land did not know what had become of the people who once dwelled there. Did they migrate? There is little evidence of that. Were the people all carried off by some plague? Possibly. The truth is not known.

Another people who left much mystery behind them are the Toltecs, the Builders. They are believed to have founded their special city of Tollán, or Tula, around the first century A.D. and then to have been driven out by the more fierce, warlike Aztecs. Much of the building and vestiges of great stone carvings and statuary formerly attributed to the Aztecs are a product of this people. It is thought that after being defeated and sent southward by the Aztecs, they reached what is now Mayan country, bringing with them their poetic symbol of the Lord of the Air and the Water—a feathered serpent. This is one of the most interesting and inspiring of the mythical animals invented by man, from the unicorn to the winged horse. It figured greatly in later Mayan art and is the theme of much stone carving.

In addition to these Indian peoples—the Toltecs, the Aztecs, and the Mayans—there were many others in the country, each with its own language, code of conduct, art, and traditions. There were the Zapotecans and the Mixtecans, who lived in and around what is now Oaxaca and contiguous states. There were Totonacas in Veracruz, and the earlier Olmecs. In the west, the Tarascans built a peaceful civilization. There was a negroid people who dwelt along the coast and who left, for our admiration and mystification, enormous basalt heads carved to look as if they are wearing a sort of helmet. These stones rest upon the earth, as a head rests upon shoulders, but how they were fashioned or moved is not known. When the Spaniards reached Mexican shores in 1517, the native peoples did not have any domesticated draft animals and did not know of the wheel. How then were these basalt heads, which weigh as much as ten or fifteen tons, transported?

Mysteries, mysteries! Mexico is mysterious, and despite

the attention of hundreds of scholars, countless puzzles remain to tease the mind, to intrigue thought, and to demand investigation.

The ancient peoples left some descendants, and in certain sections of the country Nahuatl, the Aztec language, is still spoken. Words of Nahuatl origin are part of everyday Spanish in Mexico, and some have been incorporated into other languages as well. "Tomato," for one, comes from *tomate*, or *tomatl*. "Chocolate" is another; it comes from two Aztec words meaning bitter water, *chocol-atl*. It is interesting to note that *atl*, the Aztec word for water, is also the Mayan word for water. *Atl*, then, means water, as in Atlantic Ocean. Also, while the Europeans had a mythical figure called Atlas who held up the world on his shoulders, the early peoples of Mexico had legendary figures called Atlantes who held up great weights, and Atlante figures were used to support temples on their shoulders.

Beyond quantities of fascinating material for study by historians and anthropologists, Mexico has provided the world with a long list of contributions of enormous value.

In the field of foodstuffs—always important, and more so than ever in a world with a rapidly increasing population—Mexico has contributed certain staples, among them the potato, the tomato, chocolate, and vanilla. Maize, or corn, it is interesting to note, has been found in burial caves in Mexico, and Carbon 14 tests reveal that it was grown and harvested as long ago as twenty centuries before Christ.

Herbs, plants, and extracts commonly used in medicine are almost all native to Mexico and were known to its ancient peoples and used by them. The drug digitalis from the foxglove plant; the root that provides cortisone; barks that are used to make purges or disinfectants; seeds and roots that are diuretic; and countless plants native to Mexico are part of the standard pharmacopoeia.

Some of the favorite flowers in gardens all over the world, too, have been given us by Mexico. The poinsettia, called by Mexicans the *Noche Buena,* or Christmas flower, grows wild in the country, as does the dahlia, the cosmos, the snapdragon, and countless varieties of orchid.

The gifts of the ancient peoples in art, sculpture, and architecture have been enormous. No visitor to Mexico City can fail to be impressed by the Pyramids of the Sun and of the Moon in Teotihuacán, a holy city of the Toltecs not far from the capital, where excavations and restorations have revealed an ancient city of wide streets, plazas, ball parks, and imposing monuments. The Pyramids of the Sun and of the Moon have much astronomical significance and show that the aborigines had great funds of engineering and mathematical knowledge as well as a highly developed art of stone sculpture.

Curious pyramids at Tenayuca nearby show a strange linking of the snake with worship, perhaps as a symbol of life, since it seemed to emerge from the dust. The snake figure adorns many pyramids, near the base, remaining close to earth.

The one aspect of Mexico which most intrigues scholars, and which is still the basic mystery of the country, is the great number of ruins that remain. From the primitive cliff dwellings of the north, near the United States border, to the self-contained fortress of La Quemada in the state of Zacatecas; from the niched pyramid of Tajín, with its unexplained symbolism, in Veracruz, to the enormous stone cities of Tula and Teotihuacán; in the state of Oaxaca and throughout the Mayan country in the south and southeast, it is obvious that all of what is now Mexico was once heavily populated.

Imagine, then, a Mexico covered with the ruins of cities that give evidence of early peoples and great civilizations, built layer upon layer, and above them all, the new Mexico, with its airports, highways, cities, booming industries, and modern buildings.

Imagine the whole gamut of scenery and climate: cool seas and tropical waters, jungles and pine forests, snow-covered peaks and far-stretching sandy deserts, and cities bustling with more than a million inhabitants.

Imagine a people ranging from short to very tall, from dark-skinned to the very fair, from negroid to Latin, and superimposed on this image the fact that there is no racial discrimination whatsoever.

Imagine a country where there is still pastoral poverty and where displaced city populations may live in great economic distress, and where there are also riches that reach out to the people in the form of more and more schools, more and better hospitals, a constantly improving system of social services, and a national social ideal that is striving to keep up with the fast-growing population.

Imagine all these things . . . mix into the picture exotic scents and sounds, haunting music, exciting folk dances, fiestas, and pageants . . . and you can begin to savor Mexico.

2

The Spanish adventurer who later became one of Spain's most able administrators and who is known in Mexico simply as "The Conqueror" was Hernán Cortes, a man who played a violent and dramatic role in history and left many mysteries behind him. It is known that he was born in Medellín, Estremadura, Spain, in 1485, and that he went to the University of Salamanca. Estremadura is a rough, hard country, and it bred a race of tough men. Cortes seems to have developed, besides youthful strength, an extraordinary magnetism and the power of inspiring confidence. Having been expelled from the university, he somehow got himself transported to the West Indies. When he was only nineteen, the governor of Cuba put him in charge of a fleet sent to make a voyage of discovery. Only thirteen years later, when he was thirty-two, he took another fleet of eleven vessels, about seven hundred men, and eighteen horses to Mexico, which he proposed to conquer.

This could not have been any ordinary young man. Besides a gift of command, of being able to keep men in order and carry out important missions, he undoubtedly had extraordinary courage. The Indies in those times were far more dangerous and mysterious than our own West, where so many pioneers achieved manhood and dignity early in life.

One of the most striking things about Cortes's first campaign to conquer Mexico was the fact that he ordered all his boats burned behind him. Thus, his men had to draw together, stand fast, and be loyal, for they were alone in an alien and hostile land, and they had to depend absolutely on their leader, on his resourcefulness and skill.

While it is true that the Indians of the coast were frightened of the horses—strange animals to them—of the fortresses that had sailed upon the sea, and of the cannons the Spaniards dragged with them, it must not be supposed that Cortes conquered the whole country by means of these alone. He was helped by a curious combination of factors, the most outstanding of which was that the native peoples were terrified of the Aztecs, who held the central sections of the country and ruled from their city of Tenochtitlán. The Aztec priests, who had great power, presided over bloodthirsty gods who demanded a daily human sacrifice, and the Aztec armies continuously fought neighboring peoples in order to take prisoners for the sacrifice. Thus it was that Cortes was able to acquire allies who gave him valuable information and many soldiers to add to his own, and long before he had reached the Valley of Mexico he had a considerable army.

At the same time, something else had happened that was of inestimable importance. Several female slaves were bought by the Spaniards shortly after landing, and one of them, a young woman, knew many of the native languages. With the help of a Spanish soldier who had once been a captive of the Mayans and knew that tongue, Cortes was able to begin to learn the language of the most powerful tribes and to communicate with their leaders. The woman's name was Malintzin; the Spaniards called her Doña Marina, for she became Cortes's mistress, quickly learned Spanish, took his faith, and was baptized. She was beautiful and intelligent, and without her it is certain that the Conquest, difficult as it proved to be, might have cost many more men, much more time and blood. Doña Marina was able to warn Cortes of treachery, to guide him in his dealings with the Mexican tribes, and give him confidence.

There is no doubt that she helped him because she loved him. She lived with him and bore him a son. Yet Mexicans today refer to any treacherous dealing with foreigners or even admiration of foreigners as *Malinchismo*. Any preference or admiration for foreign ways or goods over those of Mexico is also labeled *Malinchismo*. The name is unfair, for in the time of Malintzin (Malinche), Mexico was not a country but a conglomeration of warring tribes, and she, a slave, had little reason to love the Mexicans of Tenochtitlán.

This rejection of the foreign conqueror was natural enough, for the Spaniards, like other roaming pirates of their day, used bloody and unusual punishments and justified much of their violence and cruelty against the Indians by the fact that they were bringing the heathen what they considered to be the true religion.

Yet it is well to keep two things in mind. Generally speaking, people in Europe in the sixteenth and seventeenth centuries were very cruel in their treatment of criminals or of any persons considered to be of inferior class, education, or race. It took a Dickens, writing in the nineteenth century, to open the eyes of Englishmen to much of their own cruelty, and in our own century we have seen what a supposedly civilized people like the Germans could do to people they considered inferior to themselves. The Spaniards who conquered Mexico, then, should not be taken out of the context of their cruel century, nor should they be thought more cruel than the American colonists who systematically exterminated the Indians who were defending their own land.

In partial justification of the Spanish attitude, we should remember that the Spaniards brought Mexico the language that is hers today, and a culture and social organization that persist and have become deeply Mexican in feeling. The Spaniards at the same time completely did away with the terrifying religion that demanded daily human sacrifices. They did more: they brought, along with their Christian faith, an army of educators who set themselves unselfishly to teach the Indians reading, writing, music, and other arts. Little by little the Spaniards pacified the whole country as they explored it, bringing it all under a strong government which kept order, maintained peace among the tribes, and raised Mexico to the level of the great colonial countries in other parts of the world.

On the other hand, the Spaniards had a hunger for gold

and were shortsighted about other kinds of wealth com-
pared with it. And they invented the reprehensible system
called the *encomienda,* which enslaved the Indian peoples.
It worked this way: a Spanish citizen was given land
(much as our pioneers were awarded homesteads), but at
the same time was also given all the Indians living upon
that land. The Spanish landowner then became a slave
owner, his only obligation to his slaves being a promise to
baptize them and teach them the Christian faith. This system of slavery was opposed by the Spanish friars who had
followed in the wake of the conquerors, and after many audiences with the king of Spain the friars were able to put a
stop to it, though in the process they agreed to the importation of Negro slaves. There were never great numbers of
Negro slaves in Mexico, however, and all were freed in
1810, fifty-five years before our own War Between the
States, or Civil War, set slaves free.

The Spaniards brought with them into Mexico their own
type of architecture, based on the great stone fortress-
palaces, the "castles in Spain" that we have all read and
dreamed about. They also brought a kind of Moorish or
Arabic type dwelling which has a number of advantages in
Mexico. This kind of building, constructed of strong stone
walls around a central patio, could be defended from rob-
bers and mobs, and in Mexico in the days of the Colony
there were no police to protect householders. Moreover,
these dwellings, being sturdy and thick-walled, were the
safest kind of construction in a country plagued with earthquakes. Then, too, they were cool in summer and warm in
winter, and since wells were located in the central patios,
water was protected from contamination.

The Spanish family organization—a strong head in the person of the father, whose authority is unquestioned; the subjection of the sons to the parents; the strict protection of the daughters until their marriage—has come over into Mexican ways. Though in the large cities this is changing to some extent, it is still generally observed.

The rising cost of land in the large Mexican cities has resulted in the construction of more apartment buildings. Apartment living has changed much in Mexican family life, although the ideal of the chaperone for young unmarried persons still exists and is respected. While young women now are often trained for work, it is still only a minority of women who work outside the home after marriage.

Despite the impact of all these Spanish ways upon Mexico, one small aspect of Spanish thinking caused a new race to come into being in the territory. Aside from religious concerns, the Spaniards had not the slightest prejudice against marrying into Indian families. Marriages between Spaniards and Indians could always be celebrated if both partners were members of the Catholic Church. The result is that Mexicans today are a fusion of the original Spanish and the indigenous Indian races, with traces of other European blood as well, and occasionally something of the negroid, especially along the Caribbean coast. It is a hardy people, physically strong and mentally shrewd, alert, and enterprising, often poetic and very artistic as well.

The Indian peoples have had a permanent effect on taste in food, and fortunately the Mexicans have appreciated and preserved their cultural heritage from the indigenous races. The Indian corn tortilla is still widely preferred to the Spanish white roll or bread, and Indian chili is a favorite condiment on all Mexican tables and in many of their dishes. The Indian cuisine is remarkably rich and subtle, and persons who think of all Mexican food as "hot" are only partly right.

In present-day Mexican homes, even of the nonaffluent class, a wide variety of dishes is enjoyed, some of Spanish origin, like soup, *fabada* (a dish made of white beans and sausage, plus tomatoes and other vegetables), *bacalao* (dried codfish), and sweets, a great many of which came directly from the Moors and Arabs, and use honey, almonds, and cinnamon for flavoring. An endless variety of Mexican dishes are based on the tortilla in various combinations, and on stews of meat and vegetables spiced with selected chilis, of which there is an enormous variety. Mexican homes also use such contributions to the cuisine as the French *cassoulet* and *coq au vin*, American biscuits, hot dogs, hot cakes, hamburgers and ice cream, English *rosbif*, and Italian spaghetti and other pastas.

The very poor people live mostly on beans and rice, cooked with tomatoes and chili, tortillas, and a bit of cheese or egg, and occasionally meat. The tortilla, being corn, first slaked in lime and then ground, is rich in natural vitamins, and the calcium builds strong teeth and bones. The beans supply carbohydrates and some protein, and the rice, not overpolished, contributes needed minerals. There is a deficiency of protein, but the Mexican government is trying by various means to persuade the people to eat more fish, which could be provided inexpensively in abundance. However, Mexicans are touchy about their food, have never taken very kindly to fish, and even when tortillas are

19

very expensive, they still prefer them to cheap white or dark bread.

Drinks also reflect the impact of European ways on Mexican life. Mexico is famous for excellent beer, usually manufactured under the surveillance of an experienced German brew master, and is developing a sturdy wine industry, which in turn has been watched over by Spaniards. The native drinks are tequila and mescal, both distilled from the wine of the agave or cactus plant. The fresh juice of the plant, called pulque, is heavy in vitamins, and the poverty-stricken country people seem to crave it. Since the pulque ferments rapidly, however, drunkenness has been a problem. Present government policy does not permit the licensing of any more saloons or cantinas. At the same time, the cultivation of agave has been strictly limited, and the supply has been rationed. As time goes on, and the purchasing power of the people is increased and better food is available, the poor will undoubtedly tend to buy more food and will not crave the pulque.

In dress, Mexicans in the large cities resemble Europeans and Americans in cities of a similar size, but certain typically Indian articles of dress are still favored and widely used on special occasions. Women of every class wear the graceful and useful rebozo, a long scarf or stole which can be woven of silk, cotton, or wool, or combinations of all three. For the very poor woman, the rebozo is her overcoat, her shawl, and a convenient way of carrying her baby. Folded up and worn on the head, it protects from the sun; it can also be used to balance heavy jars or other burdens. The woman of the middle class uses the rebozo in her home, instead of a sweater, and often when she goes out, it is knotted around the shoulders to keep off the cold. Wealthy women have collections of beautiful silk rebozos and wear them as evening shawls.

The Mexican sandal, the huarache, is a favorite for resort wear and for sport, and the style has passed to the United States; Americans buy these sandals for wear at home and on the beach, and many men prefer them to tennis shoes for relaxing, especially as they can be worn without socks.

A typically Spanish article of clothing is still a great favorite with Mexican women and probably will never be entirely abandoned. This is the lace mantilla or scarf for the hair. Young girls wear white ones to church, to weddings and christenings, and to other religious festivities, while married ladies favor black.

The Mexican woman, too, has taken over the Spanish custom of mourning in unrelieved black. According to the degree of kinship, the period of mourning and the prohibitions that go with it are observed. For a husband, many women remain in black the rest of their lives. Others use mourning for two years or three and then go into half-mourning, or the use of some white, or a pale gray or lavender, with basic black. For a mother, one mourns a full year, though here again some men (who use the black tie of mourning) may keep it for the rest of their lives. The great Mexican composer-conductor, Carlos Chávez, put on a black tie when his mother died and has never gone back to colors.

The proper female dress for deep mourning (within a few months of the death of close kindred) is a black dress or suit (nonglossy—satin is not considered proper), worn with black stockings and shoes of a modest cut, and a plain black veil (not lace). The only jewelry allowed is a cross or religious medal, black earrings, and of course the wedding band if the woman is married. Women in mourning do not go out, except to church or on necessary errands.

This custom, which Mexican women took over from the Spanish, has served them in a peculiar way under certain circumstances. While the antireligious laws were being enforced with great severity in Mexico, many nuns were able to blend into the general populace with ease because of the great number of women in mourning dress, among whom the nuns' long black dresses and black veils were almost indistinguishable.

The Spaniards from Andalusia, who started cattle-raising and horse-breeding farms in central Mexico, brought with them their typical riding and working clothes. The men wore tight homespun trousers tucked into leather boots, leather side-protection on their trousers, their own saddles, ropes, and accouterments. The names for these things have gone straight into the Spanish of Mexico and then have emigrated to the American Southwest. The Spanish rodeo was originally a cattle roundup; the "lariat" of the West comes from *la reata*, the woven leather rope; the "Dolly Welter" (a twist of rope around the saddle horn) is from the Spanish words *darle vuelta*, meaning to wind or to loop. The sombrero, which developed a typically Mexican shape from the wide-brimmed Spanish felt, is often of straw and has come, of course, to symbolize the country Mexican, though as a matter of fact Mexicans from each state in the Republic can be identified by their straw hats—by the special shapes of the hats and the way they are worn—and these hats are by no means always of the great sweeping brim and peaked crown. The sombrero of Michoacan is elegant, flattering and dashing; the Veracruz straw hat is rather like a Homburg in shape.

Two other ideas, and the terms for them, were taken over from Spain and have become identified on this continent with Mexico. They are siesta and fiesta. The siesta, of course, is the nap after lunch, which in most Mexican homes is a heavy meal at midday. The Spanish saying is *Comida dormida, y cena paseada,* meaning "A sleep after lunch, and a walk after supper," a precept for sound health.

The fiesta is a great colorful festivity in which many people take part. More of that later, for the fiestas of Mexico deserve a chapter to themselves. Even a few pages are not enough to give any idea of their extent, color, significance, and importance in the national life.

3

Place the map of Mexico before you. If you put your hand over a long thin peninsula on the left extending from the United States border downward, what you have left is a sort of letter **J**, in reverse—heavy at the top along the border and curving upward into the Caribbean on the right. The upward-curving peninsula to the south is Yucatán. The long thin one at the left is Baja, or Lower, California. In between lies country of great variety.

The story is told that when Cortes was accorded his first audience with the King of Spain, after conquering Mexico, the king asked what the country was like. Cortes, always a taciturn man, did not try to answer in words.

Taking a sheet of parchment, he crumpled it in his strong hands and then threw it down upon a table.

"That is Mexico," he said.

The king immediately saw a country all rough mountains.

"But are there no valleys?"

"Beautiful valleys, high on the slopes, and between all the mountains."

Mexico is indeed a mountainous country; a great range extends down along the Pacific coast to the Guatemalan border, and there is another range that humps through the center of the country. These ranges run together, and the whole configuration is known as the Sierra Madre, though at its highest and roughest point it is called the Sierra Tarahumara, after the Indian tribes who still live there. This part is not yet thoroughly explored.

There are many splendid isolated peaks, too, eternally snow-covered and very beautiful. The highest is the Pico de Orizaba, which rises in the state of Veracruz. It is 18,225 feet high. Popocatepetl (Smoking Mountain) and Ixtacihuatl (Sleeping Woman) guard the Valley of Mexico. About these two beautiful peaks there is a legend which has come down from Indian tradition. The story is this:

An Indian prince was betrothed to a beautiful princess, but he was obliged to go away to war, and the word came back to her that he had been killed. She was very sorrowful, and she lay down and covered herself with a white mantle, and died. The prince, who had not been killed, returned and found his beloved sleeping—the long sleep of death. Crouching beside her, he burned incense to her memory, and there he keeps watch to this day. The Sleeping Woman is a volcano shaped like a woman, sleeping under an eternal coverlet of snow. Nearby is Popocatepetl, which means Smoking Mountain because this extinct volcano, also snow-covered, sometimes sends forth puffs of smoke. Indeed, geologists say that it might some day become active once more.

There is a cult of mountain climbing in Mexico, which has produced many climbing clubs and groups of hikers. "Popo," as Popocatepetl is affectionately called, is always being climbed, and "Ixta," which is more difficult, attracts more experienced climbers. Orizaba is climbed too, by special groups, and so is the Nevado de Toluca, another eternally snow-covered peak not far from Mexico City. Still another beautiful mountain is Malinche, in the state of Puebla; it is of such regular shape that it reminds people of Fujiyama in Japan.

Because of the great *cordillera,* or range, down the length of Mexico, the central portion of the Republic consists of a high plateau. This is where most of the important cities are located, for the Tropic of Cancer passes through Mexico just below Durango, or almost at the center of the country. Below are the tropics, but due to the altitude of the central plateau the climate in central Mexico is temperate, even cool, and with no unusual extremes, though it may grow cold enough to snow once in twenty years or so.

However, within the tropics, at sea level, along the coasts, the vegetation and climate are typical of the tropics, and where the land is fertile and well-watered, many excellent tropical crops can be harvested, such as pineapples, mangoes, bananas, and sugar.

While the northern part of Mexico is somewhat desert-like in character, there are a number of great rivers in the country, and one of the tasks of the government is building dams along these rivers at strategic spots. These dams not only store water and provide irrigation for farmland, but also save lives and property when the rivers flood, which they tend to do periodically.

The Río Bravo, called the Río Grande, is the longest Mexican river. It marks the border between the United States and Mexico, and the two countries share the expense and the benefits of a dam built to hold back its waters. In the north, the Yaqui River runs into the Gulf of California, the sea that separates Lower California from the mainland of Mexico; farther south, the Río Mayo empties into the Pacific. A great river is the Lerma, with its tributary, the Balsas. This river provides drinking water for the eight million inhabitants of the city of Mexico and its suburbs. Draining the eastern part of the country and pouring water into the Gulf of Mexico are a number of impressive and beautiful rivers: the Grijalva, the Papaloapam, the Panuco, the Coatzacoalcos, the Nazas, and the Usumacinta. The Usumacinta rises in Guatemala, flows through Mexico, and empties into the Gulf of Mexico. Only the Usumacinta has been used for navigation, to some extent, although small boats also go a short way up the Grijalva. Great dams are being built along the Papaloapam, the Balsas, and others; we will speak of these more at length later, for they are part of the picture of modern Mexico, and with these dams the Mexican government hopes to solve several of the most pressing economic problems of the people.

In the early days, when the Spaniards arrived, Mexico was still richly wooded, and the native peoples loved their forests. The Aztec Emperor took his ease in lovely parks, where tall trees provided beauty, refreshing shade, and

27

homes for birds. A remnant of this area is still the favorite park in Mexico City. Here in Chapultepec Park are tall trees, gardens, paths, artificial streams, lakes, and pleasant vistas. Another such park is the lovely Xochimilco, which means Floating Gardens. This too was devised by Aztec landscape artists as a unique kind of pleasure garden; they floated man-made islands in the canals and streams of the district, planted tall trees alongside the waterways, and kept the little floating islands blooming with every sort of fragrant and colorful flower.

As a result of the centuries-old Spanish custom of using charcoal—a custom continued until very recently—the forests of Mexico have been endangered, and the government has now made it a misdemeanor to cut any tree without a license to do so. Thus some attempt is being made to control the deforestation, which had proceeded dangerously in some states, and at the same time reforestation is beginning. But it will be a long time before Mexico recovers her true forest wealth.

There are still amazingly interesting forests to be seen and traveled through, however—some man-made and others natural, that is to say, native to the soil. In north Mexico, toward the eastern coast, in the states of Nuevo León and Tamaulipas, one may drive for hours through orange groves. The oranges grown are the Seville type, small and juicy. The American navel orange is almost never seen, because the Mexican taste in oranges is like the Spanish. Grapefruit trees, too, flourish in this section and are widely cultivated.

Farther south, in the state of San Luis Potosí, there are

palm forests, mile upon mile of them, and the high mountains are dressed in pines and mountain oak.

Mexicans cherish certain single trees that have been identified with their history. In Oaxaca the famous Tule Tree, a giant cypress, is one of the wonders of the region. The trunk is 160 feet in circumference, and the tree rises to a height of 140 feet. The tree was standing there, putting out its leaves, a thousand years before Columbus set foot on the shores of the New World.

In Mexico City is another tree that has a venerable history. In 1520, after the Spaniards had been in the city of Mexico (Tenochtitlán) for six months, apparently negotiating with Montezuma, the emperor, it became clear to the Aztecs that the Spaniards wanted nothing but gold. The Aztecs no longer believed that the Spaniards really wanted only to make friends and teach the new religion of Jesus. While Cortes was away from Tenochtitlán, defeating an expeditionary force that had been sent against him from Spain, a quiet resistance was organized. When he marched back triumphant, having routed the soldiers under Narváez sent to unseat him, there was no friendly reception from the Aztecs. The great city was silent. When Montezuma arrived for an audience with Cortes, it was made clear to the emperor that Cortes now looked upon him as a prisoner and the city as his spoils.

Before long the Mexicans attacked, and in such numbers and in such fury that they drove the Spaniards out of the city along one of the causeways built into the part of the city still known as Tacuba. The slaughter of the Spaniards was very heavy, and the story is told that the next day, when Cortes reviewed what was left of his ruined and crip-

29

pled troops, he sat and wept under a giant cypress growing nearby. The tree is called the Tree of the Sad Night, and it has been preserved with greatest care. Relic-hunters did it great damage for a time, before the tree was protected by a strong iron fence. In recent years attempts have been made to preserve its life by modern cement tree-mending methods. However, it is clear that the Tree of the Sad Night will not endure forever, so special relics of it have been taken and are preserved in the Museo Nacional de Historia.

The climate of Mexico varies as much as the altitude. The high plateaus of the central section almost never have frost, though wintry winds can make the air seem very cold at an altitude of 6,000 or 7,000 feet. In the north, in the desert areas along the United States border, great extremes of climate are usual. The thermometer may climb to 114 degrees in the summer, and there may be severe snows in winter. This section is also subject to sudden drops in temperature as a result of strong winds from the north, called *nortes*, or northers, which may occur at any time during the year, except in deep summer. In towns of the central plain, like Guadalajara and San Luis Potosí, there may be a few cold days in winter, and there may be a few hot days in summer. Generally, though, the matter of climate may be illustrated by two stories, always told visitors:

"Winter?" asks the man from Guadalajara. "Yes, we had winter one Thursday last year."

The other story recounts that a visitor took back her thermometer to the store, claiming that it was broken. "It just sticks at 79 degrees, winter and summer," she complained.

In Mexico City, the capital, and southward there is a

tropical kind of weather in that the seasons are not really winter and summer but dry season and wet season. The dry season corresponds to our winter and spring. The air is clear and bright, the temperature ranges from cool to balmy, and there is little or no precipitation, unless in the Gulf or in the Pacific there is a big storm which drifts across the mountains, causing rain for two or three days. The rainy season generally begins anywhere from mid-May to June 1 and continues steadily through September 15, sometimes lasting into October. The mornings are sun-lit and warm, but clouds begin building up by noon, and by four or five in the afternoon the first rumblings of thunder may be heard. The rain generally comes swiftly afterward, a drenching, heavy downpour, lasting from twenty minutes to an hour or two. After it stops, the whole world seems washed, clean, sweet smelling, and fresh, and no more rain need be anticipated until next day at the same time. This is particularly true along the tropical coasts and in coastal cities like Acapulco.

Ports on the Gulf of Mexico side, such as Tampico and Veracruz, are subject to three-day storms (northers), which can absolutely paralyze the city. These towns along the gulf coast are also targets for occasional Caribbean hurricanes, which start building up in September. On the Pacific side there is a bad storm once in a while, but they are rarer than the Gulf storms.

Mexico is often hit by earthquakes, the great faults seem-ing to run through the country in discernible lines. Mexico City is often shaken by small quakes, and so is the state of Oaxaca. Mexican architects, taking this fact into considera-tion as a more or less perennial menace, have learned to

31

construct earthquake-proof buildings, and there has not been any loss of life (or excessive property damage) from earthquakes for many years.

The reason for the "nervous earth" in Mexico is not merely the earth faults, but the fact that a great deal of the territory that is now Mexico was originally volcanic. Everywhere in the Republic there are evidences of great eruptions from volcanoes of the past.

South of Mexico City is a deep ancient lava bed, which has been exploited to make an extremely attractive residential section. Homes have been built to take advantage of the curious convolutions of the lava rock and are most unconventional, interesting, and personal. This eruption, from a nearby volcano extinct now for many centuries, is said to have occurred around 10,000 B.C. Yet, buried in caves far beneath the lava, scientists have found artifacts dating from ten centuries before the eruption.

Some years ago there was a rumble and a shake, and the whole southern section of Mexico felt the birth of a new volcano, which was christened Paricutín. After some months of pouring out flame and molten rock, Paricutín subsided and now is quiescent.

Mexico has many lakes, some of them large and beautiful. Perhaps the most famous one is located in the state of Jalisco, near the city of Guadalajara. This is Lake Chapala, 70 miles long and 20 miles wide. This lake wears a necklace of little villages at the shore, one of which has become a favorite retirement town for elderly Americans. This is Ajijic. The lake itself provides work and food for many people. It is filled with a white-fleshed fish, some of which are taken very small and dried, and are much appreciated in

Part of the ruins of Monte Albán at Mitla in Oaxaca, the center of the earliest Mexican civilization

The Aztec Calendar, weighing approximately 25 tons and measuring about 12 feet in diameter, was found buried under a corner of the Zocalo in Mexico City in 1790

A carved head, dating from Mayan times

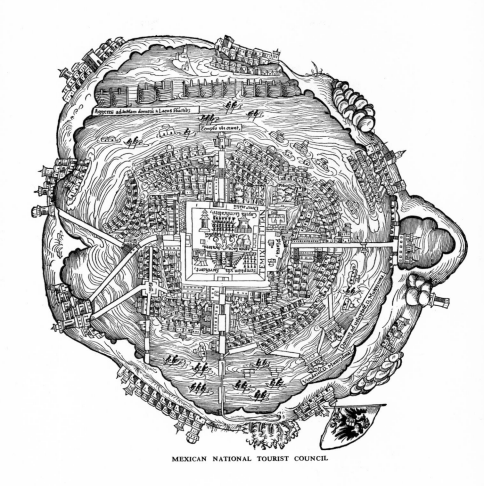

A plan of Tenochtitlán, capital of the Aztec empire from its founding in 1325 until its destruction in 1522 by Cortes. The flag at the lower right depicts the feathered serpent, part of the Mexican flag today

A nineteenth-century engraving of a Toltec king, from a drawing in a museum in Madrid

A *nineteenth-century* Spanish *lithograph* of
Hernando Cortes

The Pyramid of the Sun, built about 100 B.C.

In this Aztec drawing, Cortes and Doña Marina are depicted at right. Montezuma is seated at left

Ixtacihuatl, the Sleeping Woman, guards the Valley of Mexico

LOUIS MELANÇON

The Tree of the Sad Night, under which Cortes is said to have wept when he saw what was left of his troops after a fierce Aztec attack

the Mexican diet. At one time the lake was filling dangerously with a purple lily, which was very beautiful but a great worry because it was sucking up all the life in the water, making it difficult for fish and obstructing the movement of boats and canoes. The lily has given way now, since it has been learned that it serves as cattle fodder, and the lake is being cleared of it.

If you were to fly over Mexico on a clear day, after you had passed the northern third of the country you would begin to see many small lakes, scattered like blue jewels over the brown countryside. Around the central section there are several small towns called Lagos and Lagos de Moreno, and other names recalling their lakeside location. In this area at the end of the last century there was a flourishing local literary movement; many fine poets and essayists came from this region.

Mexico City itself was originally built upon a lake. The Spaniards mentioned this, stating that many of the houses were set upon stilts above the water and that the whole city was a maze of canals and waterways. With the growth of the city, the canals gave way to streets and the land was drained. To one side the large lake of Texcoco, which kept the temperature of Mexico City even, and provided water for many uses, was drained dry in the early part of this century; it is generally conceded now that this act was a great mistake, and every now and then there is talk of refilling the lake.

The outstanding geographical fact about Mexico (aside from its enormous variety of climates and types of terrain) is that all the important cities, except for the seacoast ports, are located at from 5,000 to 6,000 feet above sea level; Mexico City is 7,500 feet in altitude. This fact was much discussed in 1968 when the Olympic Games were due to be held in Mexico City, because a number of coaches and health experts felt that the altitude, to which most of the athletes were unaccustomed, would seriously handicap performance. However, some fourteen world records were broken in Mexico City, effectively quashing that fear. Certainly, in events requiring extreme effort, such as short runs, and jumps, the altitude had no effect at all, nor did it seem to affect the long-distance runners or the contests in which continued endurance is a factor. The matter is still under study, but it cannot be said that the altitude really affected the young, trained contestants. Many doctors do agree, however, that elderly people, or people with heart weakness or chest ailments, should not move from sea level to Mexico City without consulting their physicians.

A constant phenomenon of the skies over the central plain of Mexico and the capital city is the thick, ever-changing cloud formations. At any time of the day, between the months of March and November, one can look up into the sky and see marching armies of clouds—thick and white, and changing form as they race before high winds, far above the city streets and country fields. Flying through Mexican skies can be poetry for the same reason, and one can see castles, charging white horses, heaps of whipped cream—whatever the moment and the fancy of the observer dictate.

In the clear rainless months in the tropics the stars seem to blaze very low in the black velvet skies, but travelers feel this about all tropical countries.

That Mexican skies can be reliable for most of the year is proved by the fact that one of the world's important observatories is located in the state of Puebla, near Santa María Tonanztintla. Observatories all over the world cooperate and have divided their labors to some extent, each one carrying out a specific duty for the benefit of all the rest. The task of the observatory at Santa María Tonanztintla is to define the limits of our solar system. In the present space age, with travelers looking longingly toward planets that may be visited in the foreseeable future, this duty is an important one.

4

It is the custom of *capitalinos*, or residents of the capital city, to call it simply "Mexico." And "Everything outside of Mexico is Cuautitlan," is one of their favorite remarks. Cuautitlan is a dusty, undistinguished village.

In other words, Mexico City bears much the same relation to the rest of the country that Paris does to France. It is the center, the place where things happen, the dream of all provincials, the goal of artists and writers and hopeful beginners, whether they yearn for careers on the stage, in the movies, in politics, or in one of the professions.

Like Paris (and like Rome, London, Constantinople, and some other great cities of the world), Mexico City is a mixture of the ancient, the medieval, the modern, and the very new. When excavations were made to start building the

36

great cathedral of Mexico City, ancient pyramids were found underneath. This was in the year 1523. In 1968, when excavations were begun to build a subway system along important routes of traffic in modern Mexico City, other ancient pyramids and monuments were found. The whole city rests upon ruins of ancient civilizations which have left their own temples and edifices to serve as foundations for the new.

The city spreads out across what is now a plain, although in years past it was a lake and swamp and waterways. Toward the north are the great modern airport, factories, and residential sections which center around the beloved Basilica of Our Lady of Guadalupe. During the Revolution, the antireligious leaders changed the name of Villa de Guadalupe to Villa Madero, but so deeply is Guadalupe a part of the heart of every Mexican that the new name is used only on official papers. It is La Villa or Villa de Guadalupe to all but the bureaucrats.

The very center and heart of the city is exactly where it has been ever since the Spaniards conquered it, and it still bears the name Zócalo, which means Plaza de Armas, the central square where soldiers parade before the government buildings. Forming a beautiful square around a great paved plaza are the cathedral, the National Palace where the president holds formal audiences, the City Hall, and a fourth important national building, the government pawnshop, known as the Mount of Mercy, or Monte de Piedad. Indeed, at least once a year the pawnshop does turn out to be a Mount of Mercy when on Mother's Day (celebrated with fervor in Mexico) it is customary for the

37

wife of the president to release pawned articles to poor mothers, such articles as sewing machines or stoves.

On great national holidays, such as the Independence Day festivities on September 14 and 15, and at the end of the year, the whole Zócalo is brilliantly lighted, and it is a strikingly beautiful spectacle, each of the dignified old buildings outlined with light, shining in the darkness with a kind of general radiance.

There are a number of things that stand out at first glance when one takes a leisurely automobile tour of Mexico City. It is a city of flowers and fountains. Almost every great avenue is lined with blooming plants or is divided by a small planted garden running down the center. The city's gardeners work all year keeping the plants rotated so that something bright and colorful is constantly in bloom: gladiolas, dahlias, roses, chrysanthemums. Along some of the older streets, trees that come into blossom at some period in the year add their shade and on occasion their color. The jacaranda tree, with its purple and lavender blossoms, seems to turn the very air a romantic violet in the late spring, and the fallen blooms paint the pavement mauve in the Colonia Condesa.

Most of the wide avenues break occasionally into circles, called *glorietas*, which are liberally planted and often boast statuary and fountains too. It is remarkable that these flower beds all over the city are accorded great respect by all Mexicans. There is a fine for picking the flowers, yet one never hears of anyone doing it, not even the poorest citizen. Mexicans love flowers, and even a pitiful hut fashioned of tin cans beaten flat will display at least two or three geraniums by the front door.

The fountains of Mexico, too, give the city life and fragrance, and the poetic fancies of the Mexicans have been given full rein in the way water is used to paint crystalline designs.

Water is treasured in Mexico. The city has grown to enormous size (there are at the last count almost eight million inhabitants of the Federal District), and water for the uses of the city has to be brought from the Lerma River, many kilometers away. At the point where the water is impounded and then sent out all over the city, Diego Rivera designed a striking monument with a curious sculpture which lies half in and half out of a shallow pool of some size.

The ancient Mexicans paid homage to a water god; all over the countryside were large figures of the Chac Mool, or Lord of the Waters. Such a figure, enormously massive and weighing many tons, lay for centuries in a ravine beyond the town of Texcoco, not far from Mexico City. When the splendid new Archaeological Museum was built in Chapultepec Park, in Mexico City, the reclining Chac Mool of Texcoco was hoisted by powerful cranes, loaded onto specially reinforced trucks, and brought into the city to be set up near the entrance of the museum, where it now stands.

Curious things happened, however, when the stone Lord of the Waters was disturbed, lifted from his resting place, and transported. Rains fell in such torrents on the city, and all along the way the idol was moved, as to cause unprecedented floods. Even newspaper cartoonists published daily drawings, begging the Chac Mool to have mercy.

Among the favorite fountains of the city one should list

first those in Chapultepec Park, once the pleasure park of the Aztec emperors. There are countless fountains, following every sort of design and fancy. A second area is the Alameda or Elm Grove of Mexico City, which for centuries has been set aside as a park. Here the fountains are adorned with statuary, some of it copied from famous Greek and classical groups.

A fountain that arouses considerable tart comment from worried guardians of public morals is the Diana at the end of the great Avenida de la Reforma. The waters play in a diaphanous veil around a bronze figure of a maiden in the act of drawing a bow on her prey. The maiden herself is of such luxuriant and provocative loveliness in her nudity that there was no lack of opinion that she ought to be covered. But luckily art prevailed over morality. The Diana, triumphantly beautiful and naked, forever draws her bow above the leaping water of the fountain. Farther along Reforma is the Petroleos Fountain, an imposing bas-relief sculpture in bronze commemorating the Mexican repossession of the country's oil resources. It has become an important landmark, for it stands at the junction of important exits and entrances to the city. There are many other fountains— small, beautiful, pretentious, historic—throughout this city, which adores water.

Two great avenues of the city bisect it, Reforma and Insurgentes. Insurgentes, the longer, begins at the northern edge of the city and runs straight through it, emerging in the south, where it becomes the highway over the mountains leading to Cuernavaca and Acapulco.

Reforma, which crosses Insurgentes at right angles, begins at the western edge of the city, cuts Chapultepec Park in half, and proceeds forward to where at last it becomes, first, Juárez Avenue, and then Madero, ending at the Zócalo. Originally Reforma began at the Palace of Chapultepec and continued as far as the monument to Charles V, one of the great equestrian statues of the world, which guards the beginning of Juárez Avenue. The beautiful and tragic Empress Carlota, wife of Emperor Maximilian, designed the lovely Avenida de la Reforma and had it laid out by French engineers; it is a replica, in many ways, of a section of the Champs Elysées in Paris, and that is what Carlota intended. The avenue is broad, lined with tall trees, broken by *glorietas* with statuary and flowers, and alongside the broad walks, on each side of the avenue, are many bronze statues of great figures of Mexican history.

Reforma swoops around many *glorietas*, but there are four that are particularly important and much loved by the *citadinos*, as Mexico City residents often call themselves.

Towering above one *glorieta* is an enormous bronze statue, the Angel, which weighs many tons. It may be visited, much as the Statue of Liberty is visited in New York harbor, by persons willing to climb the 158 steps of the monument to where the statue, poised on one foot, seems about to fly away in the blue air. During a recent earthquake the original Angel was tumbled from her perch, and the monument looked denuded and sad for many months, until a new statue of the Angel was cast and at last set back into place.

Another *glorieta* is the one where the arrogant Diana draws her bow above the dancing waters of her fountain. Still another surrounds a statue of Columbus. Where Insurgentes intersects Reforma, a monument to the five great

Aztec leaders—Cuauhtémoc, Cuitlahuac, Cacama, Tetle-panquetzal, and Coanacoch—dominates the crossing.

There are other streets in Mexico that are becoming as famous as Bond Street or the Strand in London, or the Rue de la Paix in Paris. There is a cluster of short streets named for great European cities in what is called the Colonia Juárez: streets named Liverpool, Londres, Havre, Sevilla, Hamburgo, Florencia, Niza, and the like. This is called *la zona rosa*, the pink zone (for a reason not clear to anybody). It is the most elegant shopping district, where ladies can buy sumptuous and expensive jewelry and perfume, where men can purchase sweaters for hundreds of dollars, and where one can take coffee and a sandwich, or eat in elegance at nightclubs or European-style restaurants.

Then there are the streets that are connected with legend, with early history, or with some event colored by literary associations. There is the street of the Lost Child, the street of Donceles (Damsels), the street that was once the causeway along which the Spanish soldiers fought and died on the Sad Night, known first as Puente de Alvarado, later as San Cosme, and farther along as Tacuba—names that are applied to different lengths of the famous thoroughfare.

One of the most amusing legends connected with place names in Mexico is the story of the *Machimcuepa*. This word, of Aztec origin, means a somersault. The story goes that in the time of the Colony there was a very beautiful and haughty young lady who spurned all the suitors her father presented and who gave him a great deal of trouble with her pride and vanity. He therefore stipulated in his

42

will that she was to inherit his fortune upon his death on condition that she would go every year, on his birthday, to a public square and there turn three somersaults—and they were to be performed at midday, in full sunlight. Thereafter the place was known always as the Plaza de la Machimcuepa.

Mexico City of course has grown, especially in recent years, and the sections, *colonias* or *barrios* as they are called, have increased by the dozen as new settlements have been engulfed by the great capital. One of these is Villa Obregón (the Revolutionary name, but the town is still called San Angel by all residents), which was formerly an outpost, a place for picnicking, hours away by carriage from the center of the city.

Among the great *colonias* now is Juárez, which is reminiscent of the period of French influence, when many wealthy homes were being built in the French manner. This is really the heart of the elegant shopping center now, and the beautiful old homes have given way to many apartment buildings and stores, the cost of land having risen to such a degree that few can afford to keep a residence in the *colonia* today. Colonia Juárez lies on one side of the great Avenida de la Reforma; Colonia Cuauhtémoc lies on the other, and beyond, toward the north, is the dignified old section (now falling on poorer days) of Santa María la Redonda. This gives onto several poor worker *colonias* and becomes the Villa de Guadalupe, the section surrounding the beloved Basilica of Our Lady of Guadalupe.

Toward the south the *colonias* are Alamos, Narvarte, and Colonia del Valle, then Napoles, followed by Guadalupe Inn (not to be confused with Villa de Guadalupe) and San

Angel. Over toward the west, along the picturesque hills, is a palatial residential section called Lomas de Chapultepec, and nearer the heart of the city, Polanco. There are constantly growing new sections of the city as well, yet the *colonias* or *barrios* help one keep an idea of directions and of the activities in each.

Within the commercial part of the city, businesses tend to cluster together. Thus, most of the fine jewelry stores are located along Madero; shoe stores follow, one after another, along Cinco de Mayo; shops offering iceboxes, stoves, and kitchen supplies line the street of Artículo 123.

This tendency to fix locations as sections where specific purchases may be made perhaps stems from the markets and bazaars of Europe. It is also interesting to note that in Mexico City businesses tend to gravitate toward one or another of the foreign populations. For example, even today the bakeries are largely in the hands of Spaniards, either immigrants from Spain or their children born in Mexico, as is the business of making and selling mattresses and bed coverings. Hardware, however, tends to be in the hands of Germans. Americans for some time controlled the importation and sale of automobiles, but this is giving way to Mexican companies. Chinese manage small, inexpensive restaurants, and it is a saying, to indicate poverty or the state of being temporarily without funds, that one is able to buy only *un café de chinos*, a cup of coffee at the Chinese restaurant. Today, however, there are two or three excellent and elegant Chinese restaurants in the city, though extremely modest *cafés de chinos* continue to exist in great numbers.

There is an enormous and fast-growing industrial section

north and west of Mexico City, known by the name of the village around which it grew up, though now the whole section is part of the capital. This is Tlalnepantla. To the west several beautiful residential sections have been developed.

The city, which has grown so amazingly, has been spreading out toward the west and the south. On the east, the highway to Puebla has not attracted subdivisions for good homes; on the contrary, a whole city of persons who have simply squatted on the land and made themselves shelters has sprung up. This is a constant problem for the city, because these mushroom sections—without sewage, electricity, or water—are a health hazard. And yet it is difficult to dislodge many thousands of persons from their shelter.

Mexico City, with its *colonias*, its fine avenues and fountains, its parks, is also a storehouse of important historical monuments. The present cathedral, started in 1573 and finished in 1667, is said to be one of the finest in the Americas. There are many other churches of interest, among them Santo Domingo, which is still a favorite with the Spanish colony. This church, dominating a square of the same name, looked upon many of the tragic scenes carried out by the Inquisition, which flourished in Mexico in the sixteenth and seventeenth centuries. Prisoners of the Inquisition were held in cells in the building to the right of the square (as one faces the church), and were paraded through the street, in their green and yellow gowns and high peaked caps, when being brought to sentence. Executions were held here in the square.

Other imposing churches dating from the times of the

Colony are numerous in the section of the city immediately surrounding the Zócalo. These include San Francisco, the chapel of a large monastery in the hands of the Franciscan order; the Profesa, which is Dominican (and a great favorite for society weddings); and some others which have been repossessed by the Mexican government and made into museums.

At the beginning of Avenida Madero, facing the end of Juárez Street, is a white marble building surmounted by orange-colored glass domes. This is the Theater of Fine Arts, Teatro de las Bellas Artes, the seat of Mexico's National Symphony Orchestra, of great art collections, of important theatrical and operatic and ballet presentations. The Bellas Artes, sometimes referred to as "the fried eggs" (from the look of its orange domes), is the center of spectacular cultural presentations of all sorts, and there is scarcely a night in the whole year when it is dark. Offices of government sections concerned with stimulating the fine arts occupy the building as well, and give out information about painting, sculpture, ballet, opera, symphony concerts, and public concerts in parks and schools.

A curious "house of tiles" has occupied the corner of Madero Street near Juárez for years and has been successively a residence, a club, and recently a store and a restaurant. This was the original Sanborn's, an American-type drugstore and restaurant, which became a landmark in Mexico. Now a large company has bought the Sanborn name; there are branches of the store and restaurants in many sections of the city, as well as a little lunch counter which has hopefully titled itself Sanborncito's, "Little Sanborn's."

The pressure of growth of the city has resulted in the springing up of stores in the heart of each of the new residential developments, much like shopping centers in the United States. These have helped to decongest traffic and are a great boon to householders, who no longer have to go great distances to the markets.

The markets, which used to be such a picturesque part of the old city, have been ruthlessly cleaned up and lodged in modern hygienic buildings, with proper water supplies and sanitary arrangements, and are hosed down every night. This may distress the traditionalist who loves folkways more than bourgeois progress, but on the whole the clean new markets have improved the general health of the city dwellers. However, for seekers after antiques and quaint bargains, there is still the Thieves' Market (so called, and often with reason), located in the old section of the city. There are many small shops which offer baskets, serapes, rebozos, leather work, and other products of Mexican artisans, and there is a new market, where the central street of San Juan de Letrán meets José María Isazaga, which is exclusively reserved for the sale of curios and handwork.

In the southern section of the city known as San Angel are located a number of markets or bazaars which cater to artisans of the highest caliber. Painters, weavers, workers in metal, jewelers, leather workers, designers of clothes and furniture and of decorations of all sorts, rent booths in these bazaars and display their wares. They have become very popular and successful.

Mexico's museums are the most remarkable modern buildings in the city and deservedly draw the interest of all visitors. The great Archaeological Museum is a superb edifice for the housing of Mexico's treasures from the past; they have been organized and displayed with great artistry and scholarship. So ample is the government-owned treasure of archaeological riches—from the Calendar Stone to exquisite hand-hammered golden jewels—that in the cellars are stored more than is ever displayed, and it is the policy of the museum to keep the displays rotating constantly.

Located in Chapultepec Park, the Archaeological Museum is faced by a splendid new museum of modern art, with examples of the easel work of all the great painters of our time.

Down in the city, on an extension of Tacuba Street, is the new residence of the old San Carlos Art Museum, where classes in painting and sculpture are offered. The collection here is varied and valuable, the early primitives being a group of paintings that are highly appreciated by connoisseurs.

Like many enormous modern cities, Mexico City now has a cluster of hospitals, all in the same section (the Centro Médico), though older hospitals, which were financed by various nationals, still exist, such as the American-English Hospital, the French Hospital, and the Sanatorio Español, all reputable and much admired. A government hospital now of considerable international fame is the Mexican Heart Hospital, which accepts interns from many countries of the world. Other groups of modern government hospitals are located at the southern end of the city, and comprise sanatoriums for tubercular patients, persons ill

48

with nervous or mental diseases, and several children's hospitals and training centers.

Housed in a fine old Colonial building is the hospital endowed by Cortes, the Hospital de Jesús. It has never closed its doors since it came into existence, and the original endowment is now augmented from rents of all the shops on the first floor.

Typical of life in this new-old, polyglot city are the restaurants, which cater to every national taste and to every purse. It is perhaps to be expected that the finest and most expensive of the restaurants are French; wealthy *capitalinos* have always loved France, visited there, and sent their children to be educated in France when they could. (It was the practical middle class that saw that technology and future business development would be along American lines and began to teach their children English and send them on study trips to the United States.)

In a class with the elegant French restaurants are some that offer Italian high cuisine and the best of the Spanish gourmet cooking. There are excellent German, Chinese, and Hawaiian restaurants, and a few that specialize in the favorite American fare of mixed drinks, rare meats, and crisp salads.

In the lower-cost brackets are restaurants that provide the wonderfully varied and delicious Mexican cuisine, though they tend to differentiate themselves, as Norteño, (serving wheat tortillas and roast kid), Yucatecan (with dishes of venison and pork baked with strange spices), or Veracruzano (which specialize in fish and seafood). And of course, to placate the nervous tourists, who arrive for a two weeks' tour and have been thoroughly frightened about intestinal disorders, there are dining rooms in which everything has been boiled, sterilized, and disinfected.

To the south of the city is the impressive campus of the National University, the correct and full name for which is Universidad Nacional Autónoma de México, and which, as students gleefully point out, is neither national nor really autonomous. The library with its intricate decoration in mosaic—bits of native stone in natural colors which neither rain nor sun can fade—they call the "tattooed library," and an enormous stone statue of President Miguel Alemán, which has a disturbing resemblance to another world-famous personage, now dead, they call "St-alemán."

Olympic-size swimming pools and the splendid university stadium came in handy for the Olympic Games in 1968.

The university, magnet for the youth from every state of the Republic, has grown enormously, and it is now incumbent on the government to study ways and means of increasing the efficiency, the budgets, and the renown of the provincial universities, so as to hold many eager young students in their home states and decongest the university in Mexico City. Several other private universities in the city (one of them backed by American capital) absorb a certain number of students, but professional degrees from the National University are still sought by young men who wish to practice law, medicine, engineering, architecture, or other professions in the capital.

But these comments have merely listed many of the outstanding characteristics of Mexico that strike the eye or are matters of physical importance.

How is life in Mexico City? What is the special savor of the city, the feeling it gives a visitor?

Life goes on much as it does in any city of eight million or more. People tend to remain in their *barrio* or *colonia,* or the little patch of the city that has always meant home to them. They may have to journey to their work, but when they come home their interests center around the house or apartment where they live. They go to neighborhood stores, nearby movies, local parks. Generally, if working hours permit, men and working young people go home for lunch; the coffee and sandwich so usual to workers in the United States are not favored in Mexico, where long tradition demands a four-course meal if possible—a *sopa,* or starchy dish of rice or pasta; a *guisado,* of meat and some vegetable (perhaps pork with squash); *frijoles* (beans); and a sweet. The dessert is usually very simple: milk boiled with sugar until thick, or fruit ground and cooked with syrup until it is almost solid, or simple pudding. Supper, when the family gathers around the table in the evening, is not the heavy meal of the day (to which most Americans are accustomed). It is likely to be a cup of frothing chocolate and a bun, or some light dish made on a base of the corn tortilla. Movies cost only four pesos (thirty-two cents), and the price is fixed by law, so almost anyone can take his family to the movies occasionally. Most of the halls for cinema in Mexico are not luxurious, but are big, plain, and clean—that is, they are hosed and swept out with some regularity. It is the favorite diversion of all the people, though television comes a close second. People unable to buy their own television sets watch public ones in shop windows or in clubs or in the social halls of many churches, where people gather to see baseball or soccer games, great national festivals, or such occasions as the opening or the closing of the Olympic Games.

Radios are everywhere. The small Japanese transistor radio, paid for "on time," is within the reach of almost everyone. These are carried to work in coat pockets, or rest in the shopping basket of the lady of the house, and are enjoyed with devotion. Soap operas hold the attention of the women as they cook or wash, and reports of boxing or of football games (called *fut*) entertain the men.

Young people are still subject, in some degree, to the old-fashioned notions of the chaperone, though often this turns out to be a little sister or brother.

Young women in the capital city look forward to working, after their schooling, so as to have money for clothes and cosmetics, though very many of them also contribute to the household expenses. In general, married women do not work unless forced to do so. In Mexico there is still meaning in the old saying: "Work is so unpleasant that you have to pay people to do it." The important business of finding a husband may be attended to while earning some money, and then the program is to progress from acquaintance, to being accompanied to one's bus, and finally home to meet the family. Then, if things go well, the young lady may accept invitations to the cinema, or to coffee or a "Pepsi"—always if she is accompanied by someone. There must be at least three in the party. Going out alone with a young man is still not permitted until the couple are *novios formales*, properly engaged, with the consent of the two families.

Weddings are the big event in the life of any young Mexican *señorita,* and these generally take place on Saturday so that the young couple may have a honeymoon for a week or two, on the bridegroom's vacation. The weddings are as impressive and solemn as the families can afford, brides arriving in white silk with veils, and nervous bridegrooms in (rented) tuxedos. Naturally, according to Mexican law, the young couple has been married in a civil ceremony previously, for the church ceremony has no legality. Nonetheless, the young pair is considered married, in the eyes of the world and their families, only after the church ceremony.

Mexican women dress much as their American counterparts do, especially the young ones. They wear simple sweaters and skirts, suits, or semitailored dresses. It is only some of the older women who nearly always wear black dresses and plain dark veils. (Because families are large, and mourning is carried out with formal devotion, the older one grows, the more likely one is to be obliged to wear the dull black and unadorned clothes of mourning.) Hats are practically never seen, even on the most elegant of Mexican women. This custom dates from the Revolution, when it became very bad taste to use the hat, a symbol of unnecessary expense and of European sympathies. Moreover, nowadays Mexican ladies are devoted patrons of hairdressers, and they take good care of their elaborate coiffures.

It used to be a common occurrence for musicians to board buses and sing or thrum their guitars, afterward passing the hat for a few coins. Transistor radios put them out of business to some degree, however, and the new extensive *metro*, or subway system, may finish them off entirely, because no free riders will be allowed.

There is a group of young people of well-to-do families—
the kind of young people who can own cars or borrow the
family car—who go in small armies to dance and sip soft
drinks in psychedelically decorated cafés or go-go dance
emporiums, and they are faithfully reported on and pic-
tured in the Sunday press, but they are not very numerous.
Most young people are serious students or are working during the day and studying at night. The city as a whole is
busy and active. People work hard and have ambitions to
better themselves.

However, in Mexico, as in many parts of the world,
people are restless and are no longer content to eke out miserable and uncertain lives working the land, subject to
droughts, to crop losses, and to the other troubles that beset
the farmer and rancher. Mexico has not yet been able to
carry through a complete farm program. Farm loans are
not always available to the small farmer in remote districts,
and farming in many sections is still unmechanized. The
result is that a steady stream of penniless country people
have made their way to the capital in the hope of finding
some employment.

Many of these people are unemployable; others simply
cannot find a place where they can fit in. They go then and
squat on unoccupied lands, build makeshift shelters, and
simply live, partly on charity and partly on very occasional
employment that may come their way.

Faced with these hordes of homeless, the government
does what it can. If the people must be dislodged from
their huts, efforts are made to take them to other sections
where housing is being rushed through for them. The problem of absorbing the people immediately into industry is a

difficult one, however, and neither the well-intentioned government nor the charitable citizens should be judged too harshly by visitors who behold these sections of pitiful shacks. The problem is very great and is made more difficult by the constantly arriving penniless friends and relatives of the desperately poor already in "parachute" homes. (They are called *paracaidistas,* or parachutists, because they simply come to rest somewhere, without title to land or property.)

It is well to realize the magnitude of the problems facing Mexico City—a city growing far faster in numbers than in its ability to provide a water supply, communications, housing, or employment—even while one admires the rare and unusual beauty of the city itself.

Mexico City might be likened to a lovely woman, showing traces of Spanish, French, and Indian ancestry, dressed in the latest fashion and wearing jewels, but barefoot, and on the dead run, trying desperately to catch up to a rapidly retreating train, the train being a place where she can rest and draw a breath, and begin to look about.

Up to now, she is still running.

5

Other cities in the Republic, old and new, are growing as relentlessly as the capital and are receiving the hopeful tides of disappointed and starving country people.

Each has its own flavor and history.

Guadalajara, which has been called The Pearl of the Pacific, is the second largest city in Mexico and is industrializing with great speed. At the same time, because it lies within a fertile plain, it receives farm produce and meat from the surrounding countryside. Served by good highways, railways, and an international airport, Guadalajara is in close touch with Mexico on all levels; moreover, it is only two and a half hours, by air, from the American border.

The city is southern Spanish in its architecture and atmosphere. The people, called *Tapatíos*, are typically Andalusian in their beauty, grace, and animation. There was but a small mixture of Indian blood with that of the original settlers of Guadalajara, who nearly all were families from southern Spain. The young women of Guadalajara, with their camellia-pale skins, large dark eyes, and slender grace, are thought to be the most beautiful in Mexico.

Guadalajara possesses some of the finest work of the great muralist, José Clemente Orozco, who was from Jalisco; his paintings in the Hospicio de Niños are worthy of devoted study. There is also a splendid museum, which exhibits a number of canvases attributed to Murillo, and other masterpieces. And just outside the city is the village of Tlaquepaque, which is a kind of artisan settlement. Here one can find beautifully decorated ceramics, fine hand-blown glass, silver and copper work, leather articles of all sorts, and colorful woven serapes and rebozos.

Guadalajara provides all the atmosphere thought by outsiders to be typically Mexican: cockfights, bullfights, *charreadas*, or rodeos, in which all the skills of the horseman of the plains are displayed. The dress typical of the Mexican country gentleman is *charro* dress—tight trousers flaring at the ankle and high in the waist, short bolero jacket, a flowing bow tie, high-heeled riding boots, and a wide-brimmed, decorated sombrero. The costumes worn by dancers in the celebrated *Jarabe Tapatío*, or hat dance, are of the kind formerly seen in the country towns around Guadalajara, and to some degree in the city. Now, however, the *Tapatíos* are as stylish as people in any other wealthy city of its size in the world—and as completely Westernized.

The city is pious. There are many churches, and one of them houses the image of the beloved Virgin of Zapopán, which is taken out at intervals to make state visits to other churches. The social life of the city revolves around the old Catholic fiestas of weddings, christenings, first communions, anniversaries of all kinds (fifteenth birthday for girls, the receiving of professional titles for young men, silver weddings, golden weddings), and dances on great holidays. Guadalajara, so devotedly Catholic, was one of the cities that most strenuously resisted the persecution of the Church, which took place in the nineteen-twenties, and there are many authentic stories of heroism and sacrifice which occurred during the Cristero Revolution. Those who fought the government suppression of the church had a rallying cry, *Viva Cristo Rey* ("Long live Christ the King"), and for this reason they were called *Cristeros*.

The atmosphere in Guadalajara today is one of sunlit, peaceful progress. Automobiles speed down the broad, paved, clean avenues, the homes are fronted by gardens full of flowers, and the city itself carries out an efficient and humane social service to take care of any unfortunates who find themselves without jobs or income at any time in Guadalajara. One can believe the courteous, kindly *Tapatíos* when they say that Guadalajara is as near paradise as many of us can get, in this life or the next.

The object of every Mexican's patriotic devotion—besides the *patria*, which is Mexico—is the *patria chica*, the town and state of his birth. To some degree one can tell the *provincia* or section from which a man originates by his way of dress, to a large degree by his accent.

The Veracruzano seldom pronounces his *s* and tends often to turn the *ll* into a *sh* sound instead of the more customary aspirated *h*. In Veracruz the men wear white, often with black shoes, a colored scarf at the neck, and a white straw hat of a special shape: the brim somewhat rolled, not too wide, and the crown of medium height, pressed inward toward the front. It is usually unadorned. At their fiestas the women like to wear typical costume: a full-skirted dress with a fichu, in pale cotton or organdy, and a small black satin apron, lavishly embroidered.

Veracruz is a busy port, the main maritime exit from Mexico on the Caribbean side. For this reason it has seen history and has suffered from it. Political exiles hasten to Veracruz, to take boats bound for Europe; Iturbide, Carlota, Porfirio Díaz, and many another departed hastily from the port. At the same time, invaders land here, as did the Spanish in 1517 and later the French in 1862. And in 1914 the port was held by the Americans, who were hoping to discern, in the dust and rage and blood of the Revolution, some element worth backing that might be persuaded to protect American life and property.

Veracruz, which generally enjoys a balmy, sun-drenched, tropical climate, is subject to cold *nortes,* which arrive with rain and strong winds, driving people indoors and keeping them inside. Just so has history treated Veracruz. For every period of calm and peace, there has been an epoch of fury and violence. Perhaps for these reasons Veracruz has produced several of Mexico's great writers, among them the poet Salvador Díaz Mirón.

The third city of size in the Republic is Monterrey. This city has a curious history which has affected its character and position in the country. It was settled by converted Jews, under the leader Carvajal, who entered into an agreement with the King of Spain to "pacify" the dry and desertlike territory of the north, in return for safe passage from Spain for his men and their families, together with their property. Carvajal vowed to be faithful to the crown and to the state religion, Catholicism. All his followers took the same oaths, but many of them did so only for expedience. At heart they remained faithful practicing Jews, and for this reason the Inquisition pursued them. Since Catholicism was the state religion, those who lapsed from their vows were considered guilty of treason as well as of heresy.

By the second or third generation many of the Jewish families of Monterrey became, in fact, converted Christians. Their special gifts of organization, hard work, and tenacity made of their city one of the richest in the country. Its wealth is based on industry and labor, for Monterrey is the only Mexican city that has no wealthy mines of silver or gold, no fertile land, no dependable river, no lake, no help whatever from nature. Monterrey rose as the great industrial city of north Mexico through sheer determination, thrift, hard work, and foresight.

Many are the jokes about Monterrey penury, and it is popular to make fun of the north Mexican accent and attitudes. Yet Monterrey has given Mexico many of its greatest patriots—rebels all—and Monterrey has the courage to demand for itself a place in the country's economy that is almost independent of the federal power.

Monterrey's weapon, wielded to assure her independence from occasionally onerous federal control, is economic. Several times she has declared and carried out a boycott on buying, which has deprived the central government of enormous amounts of sales tax, and once the citizens even boycotted the tax collector entirely.

Although the city is so near the American border (only 130 miles away), and is admiring of and imitative of American methods and organization, the social life of the city remains profoundly Mexican. The old patterns of city life brought from Spain—surveillance of daughters, an elaborate ceremony of courtship, rigid ideas about fidelity, honor, and respect for elders—are adhered to by all classes. The devotion to work and to saving, old-fashioned virtues, plus the hardships of a severe climate—hot and dry in summer, and often bitter cold in winter—have made the people dependable, freedom-loving, and independent.

Down on the coast of the Gulf of Mexico is the old city of Campeche. This is the "Campeachy" of the pirates, and indeed the city knew depredations from Guateral (Walter Raleigh) and Aukeen (Hawkins) and others. Pirates used to assault the walled and defended city mostly to get fresh water; there was a sweet-water well near the beach, which attracted more marauders than the wealth to be taken in the city. Yet Campeche learned to defend itself. Cannons were set up alongside the city walls, facing the sea, and sometimes the pirates were driven away.

Today the city exudes an odor both salt and sweet: the drying seaweed and the quiet bay send up their salty breath to mix with the heavy-sweet fragrance of tuberose, which is grown in quantity for export to Mérida and to Mexico City, for the flower markets.

Campeche homes are usually built above a well-paved and cared-for *aljibe,* which is Arabic for a cistern. Rain water, plentiful in the summer tropical downpours, is caught and piped into the paved cellars and preserved there. On the patios above, little wells have been contrived,

61

so that buckets may be let down to take up the water in the dry season. Some homes have more elaborate systems of pumps, which pass the water by pipe from the *aljibe* through the house.

The town is famous for superior cooking, and for the good humor and charm of its inhabitants. To be *muy campechano* in Mexico is to be a delightful person.

Puebla, the fourth largest city in Mexico, has a sober, quiet solidity, a look of wealth and prosperity. The city is laid out in squares, with sections set aside for garden parks. From the time of its Colonial eminence date the many splendid churches. The cathedral is one of the most beautiful in the Americas. In the Church of Santo Domingo, the Rosary Chapel is a fairyland of entwined and laced designs, with quantities of gold leaf; it is the work of Indian artisans.

Just outside of Puebla, with its many mementos of the days when it was one of the wealthiest of Colonial cities, is the great astronomical observatory of Santa María Tonanztintla. A Schmidt camera, third largest in the world, is installed there.

Puebla has figured in many crucial battles, especially the ones that resulted in the expulsion of the hated French Empire from Mexican soil. Every year, on the fifth of May, Puebla restages the famous combat, and cannons sound from the hill above the city, where a museum and park in honor of the Victory of the Fifth of May have been built and are open to the public.

Puebla has a state university, as do Veracruz, Guadalajara, Mérida, Morelia, Guanajuato, Monterrey, and many other cities. The universities are growing, adding degrees to the ones they are presently qualified to bestow, and will be awarded more help from the federal budget.

Puebla, in recent years, has developed as an important industrial center.

Guanajuato, which grew up around the extraordinarily rich silver mines in the district, is completely Spanish in its architecture and atmosphere. The fabulously productive Valenciana mine just above the city provided wealth for the residents, and the city is endowed with many splendid churches and a beautiful theater. In the last century some of the greatest opera stars and finest theatrical and ballet troupes of the world appeared here. In recent times the Valenciana mine has been closed because it was no longer profitable to work, but rising prices for silver (as the world totters on the imposed gold standard) have made it feasible to consider reworking the famous mine once more.

Guanajuato houses one of the strange images from Spain of which little is known. It is a small Virgin, not much more than a foot high, which was brought into the city in triumphal procession, standing upright upon a drum, in 1557. The image is curious, beautifully carved, the small enigmatic face of the Virgin wearing a somewhat mocking smile. It is said to have been discovered buried, near Granada, where it had been hidden from the Moors. It dates from an early period in the Christian era and may have been carved in Africa. It was presented to the city of Guanajuato by Philip II of Spain, in gratitude for the wealth sent to the crown of Spain from Guanajuato's mines.

Another of the great cities built around mines is Zacatecas. Situated in a canyon between cliffs, the city is spectacular. Some of Mexico's most famous battles were fought around it, notably the one in 1915 in which Pancho Villa brilliantly defeated the professional soldier Huerta, and turned the tide of the Revolution.

Morelia, serene and quiet, located not far from Lake Pátzcuaro, is the seat of an old university, now the state university, which despite the tranquillity of the town has been the center of many rebellious student uprisings.

Oaxaca, called the "green city" because of the pale jade color of the stone used in much of the construction, is another Mexican city with its own special quality and personality. Despite the Spanish-type architecture and the many fine churches, today the city is Indian in its atmosphere. It is one of the few cities in Mexico that exist amid the settlements of numerous Indian peoples who have preserved to a large degree their costumes, traditions, and customs. They come into the city to attend, and to sell at, the markets, to exhibit their weavings and artifacts and their exquisitely handmade filigree jewelry of silver and gold. The local museum is one of Mexico's treasures, housing as it does the gems and priceless artifacts recovered from tombs in the great archaeological zone of Monte Albán, which has been partially excavated. The ruins of this enormous city are still to be seen on the hilltop above Oaxaca. It was a great center of advanced astronomy, art, and mathematical learning, of medicine, and of architecture.

To the north of Oaxaca is the ruined city of Mitla, City of the Dead, product of a later civilization than the one that built Monte Albán, but one rich in artistic imagination. The intricate and delicate stone carving is called "stone lace" because of its resemblance to designs made with thread.

Mérida, the "white city," is located on the Yucatán peninsula. It is clean and bright, profoundly Spanish in appearance and in many of its folkways, and yet it is in the heart of the ancient Mayan country. A center of music, with its own symphony orchestra and its own provincial university, Mérida has also been the cradle of some of Mexico's most distinguished writers.

For a long time Mérida and Yucatán had little communication with Mexico City, the capital, because of lack of railways and highways. The people were closer in spirit to those of Cuba, just across the water, or of New Orleans, which also could easily be reached by boat. Children of well-to-do families were more often sent to New Orleans or other American cities for their final education than to Mexico City. Even today, a three-way water route has been planned which would link Mérida, New Orleans, and Havana. The Castro revolution has put a stop (only temporarily, it is hoped) to that dream.

Querétaro, San Miguel de Allende, León, and other cities of the central plain, called the *Bajío* (meaning "lowlands," though these lands are only relatively low, being 5,000 to 6,000 feet above sea level), were so intensely connected with the war for freedom from Spain that the whole section is called "the cradle of independence."

Anger had been rising against the Spanish-born administrators who controlled Mexico under the vice-regency, or the crown, in the period from the Conquest to about 1800. Creoles, persons of Spanish blood born in Mexico, were passed over in all sorts of honors and activities, in favor of Spanish-born arrivals. The Indians and the mestizo had practically no rights at all, and there were many abuses.

In Querétaro, the wife of the mayor, known to history as La Corregidora (which means wife of the corregidor, or local governor), was involved in a conspiracy to revolt against Spain. Overhearing talk of a plan to quash the suspected rebellion before it could get started, she sent this news to one of the plotters, the priest Miguel Hidalgo, who was curate of a church in the town of Dolores. Deciding that the hour had struck, Hidalgo rang the church bells on his parish church and summoned freedom-loving Mexicans to rise in arms against Spain.

This cry to arms, this demand for freedom, is re-enacted every fourteenth of September by the president of Mexico, who shouts the same words from the balcony of the Presidential Palace in Mexico City, setting into motion the celebration of the "Independence Day" festivals of the fourteenth and fifteenth of September. Throughout the whole Republic, mayors and governors, too, re-enact Hidalgo's *grito*. The words of the patriot priest are immortal in Mexico.

Yet Hidalgo, the young dragoon Ignacio Allende (for whom San Miguel is named), Morelos, and most of the other heroes of that first struggle lost their lives. It was not until ten years later that Mexico at last achieved full freedom from Spain.

The towns of Querétaro, San Miguel de Allende, Dolores (always afterward called Dolores Hidalgo), and others, lie in a lovely countryside. Today these towns see tranquil days as their people prosper from house industry, which flourishes in the region. Near the town of León, at almost the exact center of the Republic, stands the enormous Christ of Cubilete, topping the highest peak in that part of the country. It is an impressive image, showing Christ with outspread arms, in the attitude of "Come unto me all ye who are heavy laden," and countless pilgrims make their way up the mountainside to hear mass at dawn there, at the feet of the image, on the day of Christ the King, the last Sunday in October.

The constitution of 1917 accords great strength to the federal administration of Mexico, and the states suffer a certain loss of sovereignty. For example, governors are often appointed, rather than duly elected. Yet the spirit of independence is strong in Mexicans, and the *patria chica* is an enduring loyalty in the heart of every Mexican.

Although it may seem to be a statement stronger in wish than in fact, yet it is largely true that sports competitions today drain off a good deal of the ancient rivalry between sections. And the rise of interest in sports—participation in sports, and public devotion to them—is one of the outstanding facts in the history of the last twenty years in Mexico.

6

Unless one looks at the history of Mexico, and notes the tides of enslavement that have engulfed the people from time to time, it is difficult to appreciate fully the passionate Mexican devotion to the ideals of liberty and independence. Few people have fought so hard, and shed so much blood, to achieve these.

The ancient peoples lived in terror of other tribes in the region. It was an era of fierce warfare, partly for territory, and partly for religious reasons. It was the custom to take one's prisoners of war for the purpose of propitiating the bloodthirsty gods with human sacrifices. It was only in the last century or so before the Conquest that Toltec descendants and Mayans no longer made war to acquire human victims for the gods. The Aztecs did, and were feared and hated generally.

Then the Spaniards came. They were impressive, those white-skinned people with golden hair, mounted on great snorting beasts, wearing clothing faced with glittering metal plaques that turned away arrows, and carrying with them terrifying arms that spit fire and could fell men fifty paces away.

The coastal tribes and later the Tlaxcaltecans allied themselves with the mysterious, powerful strangers, because they feared the Aztecs more. The Aztecs themselves, after spies had brought back many disquieting reports to the Emperor Montezuma, decided to receive the invaders with courtesy and gifts and try to find out their intentions. When it became clear to the cautious Aztecs that the Spaniards were after gold and would stop at little to acquire it, they dropped their pretenses and began a stubborn resistance. In the end, as we know, they were completely overcome, and the sacking of the great city of Tenochtitlán began. The Spaniards spread out and began systematically subjugating the territory, setting up barracks and exploiting the mines (which turned out to be mostly silver mines, after all, but still of immense value to the Spanish Crown).

It is important to realize that it took the Spanish troops many long years to "pacify," as the saying goes, the peoples who opposed them; in the central-northern plain the savage Chichimecas were never completely defeated. Like our own Indians of the Great Plains and the West, they were either exterminated or absorbed into the social pattern through intermarriage.

But in many other parts of Mexico, where the Indians were more docile, the *encomienda* system gave to favored persons certain lands, *as well as all the people living upon those lands,* their only obligation being to see that the Indians were Christianized. Hatred of the Spaniard, or *Gachupin* (probably coined because of a similar Indian word meaning "spurred"), persists as one of the instinctive emotions of many Mexicans today.

In 1810 a struggle to gain independence from Spain began. It involved many patriots and leaders, the first two precursors of the Independence movement being Hidalgo and Morelos, both priests. They were fought, eventually captured, and executed. Independence was achieved in 1821.

Yet all those who had shed their blood in the eleven-year struggle for freedom had suffered in vain, it seemed, for the first Mexican Congress, called in 1822, was prevailed upon to set up a regency and to proclaim Agustín de Iturbide as emperor.

Iturbide, with his pretensions and his luxury-loving followers, did not last long. The empire was overthrown, and he was shot in 1823. The United States of Mexico were proclaimed, and an attempt was made to fit Mexico into the pattern of free republics in the New World. A new, power-hungry, gifted, and evil man had risen to power with Iturbide, however, and he continued to embroil Mexico in difficulties, among them war with the United States. This was General Santa Anna. Mexicans expelled him three times from their country and repudiated him publicly, and yet he was able each time to return, to find followers, and to take up arms again.

American troops under General Zachary Taylor entered Mexico in 1846, and did not leave until 1848.

It was Santa Anna who, after his defeat at the hands of the Americans, sold an enormous portion of Mexican territory—Texas, Arizona, New Mexico, and California—to the United States, for a trifling sum. The whole thing galled Mexican patriots, as it would if, let us say, Canada rose in arms against the United States and ended up purchasing Michigan, Minnesota, the Dakotas, Ohio, and Illinois.

Residents of the United States have no experience to guide them in how they would feel if they had been humiliated and their territory wrenched from them because of the ineptitude of a leader who had been repudiated time and again by his own nationals.

Again, poor Mexico was not "free" for very long.

Now there was a steadily rising swell of resistance to some of the entrenched privileges and reactionary ideas of the minority that controlled power and wealth in the country. The Catholic Church, which owned vast tracts of land, urged the wealthy upper classes to fight for the Church's privileges. But the opposition grew in strength, and under President Comonfort, in 1856, Mexico decreed the open public sale, at assessed value, of all lands and property held by the Church. A few years later, after Benito Juárez was elected, the reform laws broke the material power of the Church forever.

Benito Juárez was a liberal, sympathetic to all the tides of revolution running in the world. He was also a Mason who had close ties with other Masons in the world. At that time Masonry took a vigorous part in politics in many countries, and the men who took Masonic vows were opposed to all influence by the clergy. In Mexico, Masonry has continued to play a strong role in politics and is always allied with liberal groups against conservative Church groups.

But there was a furious conservative party ranged against Juárez, and the Church and the Catholic clergy took their part. These were the two groups that were drawn up against each other, ideologically and otherwise, at the time of the French intervention in 1861.

Napoleon III sent Maximilian, archduke of Austria, to rule Mexico after French troops had occupied many Mexican towns. The conservatives, the Catholic Church, and the royalists in Mexico were delighted to receive Maximilian and his beautiful Carlota. But Benito Juárez, the quiet, studious, stubborn Indian who had been duly elected president, did not turn over his power to the well-meaning but misled Maximilian.

Juárez and his party steadily and courageously resisted the French. At last they were defeated, Maximilian was executed, and in 1867 poor Mexico was once again dreaming of a republic and of freedom from foreign armies.

One of the soldiers who had helped drive out the French, General Porfirio Díaz, was then elected president. He was a man of many gifts and a hero to the people of Mexico at the time, but he was persuaded to allow himself to be elected time and time again. His friends and followers entrenched themselves in rich and important posts. "The old man," as he began to be called in what was becoming a more or less benevolent dictatorship, resisted making any serious reforms of the enormous hacienda system and of many other abuses that had begun to be apparent.

Besides, and in this he was certainly justified at first, Don Porfirio had awarded a great many concessions to

The Poets' Walk, Chapultepec Park in Mexico City

Zocalo, the main plaza in Mexico City

Xochimilco, the Floating Gardens, in Chapultepec Park

Chac Mool, the Mayan Water God

The Diana Fountain in Mexico City

Reforma Avenue, the main thoroughfare of Mexico City, bisects one of the city's numerous glorietas

Madero Avenue in Mexico City. The tile house at the left is the original Sanborn's

La Merced, the great indoor market of Mexico City

Native markets in villages are a source of news as well as food

Left: Girls are still wooed by serenades at their windows, although the custom is disappearing in the large cities, especially the capital

Right: A simple wedding in a country village

foreign companies in order to assure his country railroads, exploitation of oil resources, mines, and many other needed materials and services. I say "at first" because few foreign capitalists wished to invest their money in war-torn Mexico, with its tendency to throw up warlords and redeemers at intervals, without promise of many special considerations and without contracts for a hundred years or so. In this way they thought they might be able to make their risk pay dividends sooner or later.

But again Mexicans felt that they were being exploited by little groups of arrogant foreigners; this had been the bitter lot of Mexicans ever since the Conquest. Don Porfirio grew older and older in his post as president and would not leave his seat of power. The grumbling rose, the opposition found words to use as exhortations, and at last the people rose in arms under many leaders, all over the Republic. The cries were "Land for the man who works it," "Effective suffrage," "No reelection," and "A new constitution."

All this was resolved (after terrible struggles and years of near chaos), and it seems that Mexico is now bound on a peaceful course, under a series of elected presidents who are civilians, beginning with the election in 1946 of Lic. (Attorney) Miguel Alemán.

The facts related above hang on the names and careers of individuals, as history so often tends to be written; but it should be remembered that millions of simple civilian people lived through all these upheavals, tried to keep going, to raise their families, educate their children, get their daughters married, and provide for their old age. Their sufferings and troubles were severe, and almost continuous. Is it surprising then that many Mexicans still look askance at any evidence of foreign influence in Mexico, and in general dislike any foreign element that seems to be growing in power, wealth, or privilege within their country? Mexicans do not have a sentimental myth of the "melting pot" in their history, and foreigners in Mexico have meant only trouble of one kind or another, and usually violence, for almost four centuries.

This being so, it is remarkable that there is little if any race prejudice in Mexico. Perhaps the subtle and distinguished Indian civilizations that the Spaniards encountered are partly the explanation for this. Today in Mexico race prejudice is almost nonexistent, although it is true that there exists a certain amount of snobbish prejudice based on economic status. But this seems to be general in the Western world.

Mexicans do have their private jokes about foreigners, and in cartoons foreigners can be recognized by the accepted caricature of each nationality. The Spaniard is portrayed as short and fat, with a heavy line of "five-o'clock shadow" almost up to his eyes; he is generally wearing a tight little beret (the Spanish *boina*) and smoking a cigar. The Englishman is shown in the long-accepted fashion, wearing a monocle and a walrus mustache. The American is portrayed in two versions: the male tourist, wearing a flowered shirt and many cameras, and a big straw sombrero; and the female, usually young and pretty, with blond hair in a ponytail, the shortest of miniskirts or shorts, and Mexican huaraches. It is, in a way, a kind of gentle forgiveness of the *gringo*, this recognition of his love for Mexican things and Mexican clothes.

The Mexicans, though, are not a bitter people. They have

always been able to laugh, to caricature, and to make jokes about themselves. There is a caricaturist in Mexico City who has devised a series of typically Mexican characters in his cartoons, which are recognized and laughed over by Mexicans everywhere. They are El Charro Matías, portrayed as a fat *charro*, or country squire, in his big sombrero and tight velvet pants, always rushing about trying to get onto some successful bandwagon and always arriving too late; and Don Gastón Billetes (which means Mr. Spend Money), who is shown with a large diamond ring on his nose, and who is full of all the pretensions and stupidities of the *nouveau riche*. This gifted caricaturist is Abel Quezada, and he exerts a powerful influence on public affairs, for, perhaps due to an innate sensitivity and to the years of trouble, Mexicans themselves are unable to bear ridicule from others. It is their Achilles heel.

7

History too often is told as a series of events precipitated by personages. In some ways, of course, it is just that. Yet the type of history that stresses broad sociological and economic and geographic movements is also true—but it is not the whole. History is lived by people, by simple souls who endure whatever difficulties the times present, who occasionally know what is happening but more often do not, and who struggle with the daily problem of how to earn a living—food, a roof, and clothing—no matter what world-shaking developments are taking place politically around them.

This has always been so in Mexico, where even during the Revolution in our era (1910 to about 1940) people had no general access to daily news. The intense preoccupation with world events, with the personalities of leaders and what effect they might have upon others, with racial and economic movements, which is part of Western daily psychology, due to television and radio and newspapers, is a development of very recent date.

What was life like in Mexico in past epochs? We have some clues to the taste and rhythm and savor of life in reports from eyewitnesses and in details that appear in poetry and novels of each century.

Before the Spaniards came, countless civilizations rose and fell in the land now called Mexico. Many were sophisticated and poetic; others were less so. When the Conquerors appeared, the Aztecs had been in control of the central plain for almost two centuries. They were late-comers, strong and aggressive, and they were enthralled by a bloody religion requiring daily human sacrifices. They made themselves feared and hated far and wide.

Yet they had many admirable qualities. Due, alas, to the religious principles of some of the first friars and Catholic prelates who came to evangelize the country, most of the literary and historical work of the Aztecs was burned. Great heaps of their beautifully painted and inscribed scientific and poetic work were put to the torch by Archbishop Zumárraga in Mexico City and by another churchman in Yucatán. It is popular nowadays to characterize these acts as vandalism of the worst kind, resulting from abysmally narrow fanaticism.

But it is unfair to judge people out of their time. The Aztecs were terrified of their gods and believed sincerely that only by daily sacrifices of living hearts could the gods' fierce destroying anger be appeased. The Christian friars thought, equally sincerely, that they must be preserved from all contact with those same gods and from books and literature that mentioned them.

Tolerance is a delicate plant which seldom flowers into true appreciation of differences. It is rare enough in our day; in the sixteenth century it simply was not present anywhere—not in Spain, not in England, not in Mexico.

We now know that the Aztecs had a rich body of poetry and drama which revealed them as a sensitive people, capable of great tenderness and inclined toward a gentle melancholy in their daily life. Like many other somewhat primitive people, they worked seasonally, cultivating corn, weaving, working stone, building, and carrying out the simple commerce of their days. Young boys were taught by temple priests, and many of them were prepared for the priesthood, or selected for military duty. Young girls learned the arts of cookery and embroidery and decoration. Marriages were arranged, families lived and suffered and prospered, enjoyed happy times, and died. Pestilences carried them off, wars killed and maimed the young men, beautiful maidens were chosen for the royal house or were sacrificed to the gods. Yet the Aztecs had great days of dancing and feasting and idleness at regular intervals, especially when according to their calendar a new century was to take place. (This happened every fifty-two years, with a few days left over. These leftover days were times of greatest religious frenzy and ritual.)

The people had no draught animals, and they themselves carried heavy burdens, supporting them on their backs, bracing them with wide bands of cloth across their brows. Bent over, they jogged or trotted and were able to cover considerable distance. (Even today, in some parts of Mexico, one may see poor people transporting furniture or stacks of birdcages or other objects in this way.)

They were water people, used to water and living on and above it. Tenochtitlán was situated upon and around a lake. The streets were canals, and much barging was done, many canals having been constructed especially to permit the moving of foodstuffs quickly into the city.

Imagine the quiet city: barges and canoes propelled with silent oars and poles, no engines sounding anywhere, no exhausts, no screaming brakes, no jets overhead, no roar of traffic. Tenochtitlán must have had many charms, but a soft quiet could have been one of the most noticeable.

The houses of the common people were small, often with stone sides and thatched roofs. The great pyramids were temples, and there were outstanding public buildings too, and ball courts and central plazas where games were played and ceremonies were conducted. And all around was the sound and smell of water, the shade and the sweet air from many trees.

Soldiers, in their battle dress of padded cotton, carrying shields made of tin and layers of stiffened cloth, could be seen marching away on their endless campaigns. Priests were carried through the city on litters, awful in their masks, with their imposing feather headdresses, and members of the royal court were seen at great ceremonies, in elegantly embroidered robes and golden jewels.

The Aztecs worshipped the Sun and believed that creation took place in recurring waves, with the birth of new suns. Their myths and ceremonies were full of a rich imagination and nobility.

After the Conquest, the life of the people changed in many ways. Country residents found that they were literally enslaved to the Spaniards who acquired their lands. Some of the friars worked hard for their native charges, taught them well and appreciated their subtle and unusual gifts. Among these was Motolinia, who was much beloved by the native Indians because he called himself "Poor Man" and went about serving the people. Another, Fray Pedro de Gante (a Belgian friar, it would seem, from his name, which means "of Ghent"), was an educator and he did much to establish schools for the Mexicans. Still another, Sahagun, took the trouble to learn the Nahuatl language and to translate the scriptures into Nahuatl.

In the first years after the Conquest, many friars set the pattern for life in Mexico for years to follow. They found a people already greatly skilled in building and in the working of stone; under the direction of the monks, great fortress-churches were erected by the natives, where they were protected, Christianized—and yes, all too often, sadly exploited for the benefit of the Spanish landholders. Though some of the friars were callous with their charges, it seems that on the whole they did their best, and many are remembered to this day with love and gratitude, among them Fray Bartolomé de las Casas, Motolinia, and Vasco de Quiroga.

It is not generally known that the Spanish missionary monks taught the Indians music and directed choirs, so as to carry out the extensive musical liturgy of the Church, with enormous success. Records reveal that there were many excellent musicians among the Indians, who learned quickly, and more than a few native Mexican composers, who began composing masses, often using themes from their own folk music. Not many of these fragments of composition remain, due to the anti-church movements and violence of one sort or another in the last century and in the twentieth. Often church libraries and music were destroyed when churches were sacked.

Under the viceroys, Colonial Mexico became a country with a suppressed native population, living under the domination of a strong alien race. Spanish became the official language, for the Spaniards were never good linguists and they turned most of the native names into something resembling Spanish. For example, Cuauhnahuac, meaning "near the woods," sounded to the Spanish like *cuerno de vaca*, or "cow's horn." Cuernavaca has become, then, the official name of the town.

Another example of Spanish lack of subtlety in language is the manner in which the Spaniards decided that the apparition of the Virgin, near Mexico City, in 1531, was that of Our Lady of Guadalupe. They knew this name from Spain, for there is an image known as the Virgin of Guadalupe in Estremadura. The Indian boy to whom the apparitions of a lovely lady of his own people appeared, promising protection and asking for a church, was Juan Diego. When he was told to learn the name of the lady who appeared to him, he reported that she was Coatashupe, which means, in Nahuatl, "She who treads on the serpent" (of evil). Coatashupe sounded like Guadalupe, and to this day the dearly beloved patroness of Mexico and the Americas is known as Guadalupe.

During the Colonial period, Spanish crown troops were constantly busy pacifying outlying sections of the country, trying to make them safe for colonization and for exploitation, especially the mines. Yet in the capital, and to some degree in other cities, there was a lively intellectual life.

The viceroy's court was the magnet for brilliant misfits from Spain, many of them rebels of one sort or another against the rigid court life of the day. A succession of mysterious and romantic characters appear, like streaks of lightning, in the dark history of those days.

One was a strange Spaniard who called himself Gregorio López. He arrived a few years after the supposed death of the son of Philip II, the tragic "Don Carlos" who had been betrothed to Elizabeth of France. When Philip II set eyes on his son's fiancée, he, who had been recently widowed, married her himself—and this despite the strong rumor that Don Carlos was in love with his prospective bride. Apparently this caused the young man to defy his father and, in the ominous Spanish phrase, "to lack respect." The result was that Don Carlos was put in prison, where the public supposed him to be mentally ill. (This would not have been hard to believe, for there was a strain of madness in the Spanish royal line, beginning with Philip's mother, the ill-starred "Mad Juana," or "Juana la Loca," who lost her mind when she lost her handsome young husband.) Later, word was given out that young Don Carlos had died in prison.

The fate of Don Carlos has become one of history's mysteries—like that of England's Edward V and his brother, the little princes murdered in the Tower of London; Marie Antoinette's son, the young dauphin; and others who disappeared under mysterious circumstances, leaving the way open to possible impostors who later claimed their identity.

Some whispered that Don Carlos had been poisoned; others reported that he had died in an excess of mad rage. There was also a curious murmur that he had been allowed to go free, to the New World, but with a new name and under promise never to reveal his true identity.

In any case, the mysterious Gregorio López landed at Veracruz and was at once welcomed into the household of the viceroy in Mexico City. Gregorio was handsome and evidently of noble lineage. He knew many languages, the arts and sciences of the day, and courtly customs. He was taciturn, however, and withdrawn, and no one got to know him very well. Tiring of court life in Mexico City, he went to Zacatecas, where the silver mines were in heavy production, a great tonnage of silver being shipped yearly to the crown of Spain. This unknown young man, untitled, who had been instantly taken into the viceroy's court, was as instantly made accountant at the silver mines. Surely he had some powerful patron. Perhaps even the King of Spain? No one ever knew.

Then the young man wearied of the life in Zacatecas. Or could it be that he was sickened by the way the Indians died under their Spanish masters, working in the bowels of the earth? Don Gregorio, all agreed, was a truly Christian and tender-hearted man. He left and went into the countryside to live as a hermit, unafraid of the fierce Chichimecas, who were still being harried by Spanish crown troops. These same soldiers came across the hermit one day and wrinkled their noses at his effluvia and his long beard and wild hair. One of them said, "Who are you? You look and smell like a dead man!" To this coarse greeting Gregorio answered gently, "I am what you say. In truth, I am a dead man."

It is known that he later entered a convent in the state of Michoacán, where he devoted the rest of his life to scholarly studies and to prayer and meditation. Who was he? Don Carlos? Or, as some suggest, an illegitimate son of Philip II? No one knows.

There was also, in this Colonial period, a beautiful young woman who, in an age when only men were educated, educated herself. She learned to read at the age of three; by the time she was eight, she had taught herself Latin, in order to be able to read all the books in her father's library. Sent to the viceroy's court, she was protected by the wife of the viceroy, Doña Leonor, marquesa de Mancera, and there she wrote plays in verse, for the amusement of the court. And she studied. She became an expert in mathematics, in music (she played several instruments, and composed), in physics (alone, by her own experiments, she worked out several physical laws), and in many languages (though not in English). She entered a convent—as a result of an unhappy love affair, it is said—learned much theology, and was bold enough to argue with distinguished princes of the Church. She became one of the most delicate, profound, and perfect of poets in Castilian, and is still so considered to this day. The little Mexican girl, Juana Asbaje, became Sor Juana Inés de la Cruz, known to all Latin America as the Tenth Muse.

Portraits of Sor Juana and of sad Don Gregorio may be seen in Mexico City, and one can muse for many hours over these faces—both young and both beautiful, one sad, one controlled, both proud and self-contained and secret.

There were other personages in those days, of remarkable qualities. Fray Bartolomé de las Casas, the apostle of the Indians, made many trips to Spain to try to free the wretched natives from the wickedness of the *encomiendas*, and he succeeded at last.

In addition to the soldiery, which arrived steadily from Spain and marched clanking through the streets of Mexico and then forth to "pacify" (what a curious use of the word!) the people, returning broken and maimed and hurt to the capital, there were the sycophants who crowded into the New World in the hope of getting rich on crumbs that fell from the viceroy's table. And there were the usual traders and merchants who began to traffic in leather, foodstuffs, clothing, and all sorts of imported goods from Europe. Over all hung the heavy shadow of the Inquisition, which was established in Mexico in 1571.

The Inquisition was terrifying because it was a secret body, and because anyone could denounce anyone else—anonymously. Thus the genuine function of the Inquisition was obscured by the thirst for revenge, the cruel calumny, and the envy to which any anonymous person could give vent by denouncing the person of whom he was envious. The victim was not permitted to know of what he was accused, or the name of the person who had accused him.

Yet the Inquisition had, in those days, a duty which we should keep in mind. It was not merely a company of sadistic torturers, as the "Black Legend" would have us believe. In those days Spain, like the other countries of Europe, had a state religion. England had one; so did France. So did the Scandinavian countries—and they still have one today, as does England, insofar as the ruling family is concerned—and Israel.

Every Spaniard entitled to defense by the king's armies had to be a loyal Catholic. No one was permitted to emigrate to the New World, there to be protected by the armies of the crown, unless he took an oath of allegiance to the throne of Spain and to Holy Church. It was a sort of loyalty oath, about which we have heard arguments even in our own time. Having taken this oath, if a man broke it and conspired against the throne *or against the Church*, he was considered a traitor and subject to the laws for dealing with traitors. The Inquisition was an *inquiry* into the matter of any denunciation. If the person accused was thought to be merely misguided, and could be brought back into the faith, he was paroled into the custody of a priest for instruction, and in Mexico he was sent to work in the hospitals for the wounded soldiers during the time of his probation. If the person was openly rebellious, or if he slipped back once more into secret practice of another religion, he was tried again, and if considered incorrigible, he was executed, usually by burning at the stake.

These burnings, or *autos da fe*, of course, horrify us. But again, it is not good historical thinking to remove Mexico from the framework of history of her day, and judge by present-day standards, any more than one does this when speaking of England during the time of Elizabeth I, or of Germany during Luther's day. It is the peculiar and saving grace of our own epoch that, although the world can still be cruel beyond imagining (witness Germany under Hitler, and Biafra under her own blood-brothers, the Nigerians), at least most of us are repulsed and horrified by cruelty. Maybe some day the whole world can be taught kindness. It is something to hope for.

Mexico was no more kind than any other country, but also no more cruel.

The Inquisition, which concerned itself very often with "relapsed Christians," or "Judaizers" (persons originally of the Jewish faith who had changed over to Catholicism and accepted baptism), brought to the New World another mysterious and fascinating personage. He was called Dr. Morales by many, and he went about encouraging Jews who had professed Christianity to return secretly to Judaism. Naturally he was pursued with a great hue and cry by the Inquisition, which never could lay hands on him. At the same time his reputation grew. He was a great healer, and one heard of him now in the north, now in Veracruz, now in Tampico, now in Mexico City. He was learned in many languages and in many sciences. He was, said many, a hypnotist and a sorcerer; he could disappear and reappear at will. Gradually the belief became prevalent that he was the Wandering Jew himself, and that the Inquisition would never catch him. And it never did. A person said to be the same Dr. Morales died quietly in his own bed in the Jewish section of Venice. Was it the same mysterious personage? We trust so.

Here, a word about the "Black Legend." It was while I was studying Latin American history at Stanford University that I first heard about the Black Legend. Professor Percy Alvin Martin, an electrifying lecturer, averred that the deep subconscious basis of mistrust between North Americans and Latin Americans was rooted in that curious historical attitude.

The Black Legend (I do not know who first characterized it thus) is as follows: Back in the sixteenth and seventeenth centuries the two great European rivals were Spain
and England. They were rivals on the seas, rivals for colonial power, and antagonists in the bitter struggle between
the Catholic Church and the forces of the Reformation.

The United States, being an inheritor of the history and
attitudes of the English-speaking peoples, was heir also to
the hysterical hatred of Spain which boiled up in England
during these two centuries and was perpetuated in historical writing, state papers, and documents of the time. Thus,
in the Black Legend, Spain became a symbol of cruelty, the
Spaniards the most bloodthirsty and hideous of conquerors, their religion fanatically subservient to Rome, and the
Spanish Inquisition the most iniquitous of human institutions.

Meanwhile, in Spain (though this did not affect the
thinking of English-speaking peoples), the English were
considered to be a treacherous and lying race, hypocritical
and money-grubbing, a nation of pirates, faithless to their
religion.

The Spanish called Walter Raleigh a pirate; the English
knighted him. The English called the Spanish "Papists"
and foamed at the mouth when discussing Catholicism; the
Spanish raged and thundered at the "heretics."

The Spanish Inquisition, which was an arm of the civil
government, looked upon heresy as treachery to the state,
for the official religion of the state was Roman Catholic. In
England, the official religion, under Elizabeth I and later
monarchs, was Protestant; Catholics were pursued like

spies and tortured as hideously as it was the custom to torture the wicked all over Europe in that day.

The Inquisition in Spain held secret trials and listened to anonymous denunciations. In England, however, men suspected of heresy or treachery were summarily executed without trial on the command of the sovereign.

In other words, those were terrible and cruel days, and there is actually very little choice between the two countries and the two peoples as far as "perfect behavior" goes. And yet, among English-speaking people, the Black Legend of hatred for Spain has persisted, while in Spanish-speaking countries it has been enormously difficult to eradicate a deep distrust of any English-speaking Protestant.

Meanwhile, Mexico was beginning to develop the hacienda life in the country that was to characterize it for a hundred years or so. Enormous ranches in the countryside, many of them lands granted by the crown to some special favorite, or for some service or other, began producing wealth, using as labor the miserable natives who had to work as they were bidden, or starve. Sugar haciendas grew up in the tropical lowlands, enclosing mills for grinding and boiling the sugar, and the elegant homes of the owners and overseers, the whole surrounded by high stone walls which could be defended by armed men, for every hacienda was a fortress. It was also a self-contained and self-sustaining community, and never lacked its own chapel.

In the north the haciendas produced grain and cattle, fruit, corn, and beans. In the south, coffee plantations began to prosper. But all were like small city-states, with their own constabularies, their own company stores, sometimes their own banks. While this led eventually to conditions that seemed unbearable, for a time the hacienda life met a need, and a rich folklore grew up around it.

Most of the arts of the cowboy were developed on the haciendas in the north, where cattle became an industry. The cowboys, or *vaqueros* (from which comes our Western expression "buckeroo"), caught the wild horses and tamed them, and taught the tough, fleet little creatures to help herd and to cut out single animals from the herd. They taught the horses to stand firm when the half-wild cattle were roped to be branded. From that time came our own Western legend of the life of the range—from the sad songs sung to the guitar around a campfire, to the words having to do with the nomadic life of the cowboy. Words moved from Mexico to the American Southwest. "Chaps" is an Americanized short version of *chaparreras,* the word for leather or wooly trouser protectors for riding through brushy country; pinto became "paint" horse (a spotted horse); a bad "ombre" meant, of course, a bad *hombre;* and a *lazo* became a "lasso," or even a "lass."

The accouterments, too, of the Mexican cowboy and of the Mexican country gentleman—who was, in the literal Spanish sense, a *caballero*—were taken over by our own Westerners. The broad-brimmed hat, the knotted scarf at the neck, the tight riding-trousers and short jacket, the high-heeled boots—all were standard wear in Mexico, and the style came directly from southern Spain, where there are cattle farms.

The traditional courtesy and defense of women, practiced in our own Old West, were a blend of the delicate manners of the Southerner and of the Mexican, who is always punctilious.

There were wonderful fiestas in the old days, on the great haciendas. People came to visit for weeks at a time; weddings were occasions for great reunions, with dancing and feasting for days, and religious holidays were celebrated with fervor. In those old times, Mexican ladies had many duties, for they were in charge of all stores of food and had to portion them out, not only for the great house, but also for all the workers and their families. They were perforce nurses, with some knowledge of first aid and much esoteric wisdom about herbs and teas and poultices. They were guardians of morals, watching over their workers with eagle eyes, and marking for weddings and christenings all those in need of the same, whenever a priest could be found and brought to the hacienda. They were designers and dressmakers, for they made their own clothes and also the ruffled linen shirts and fine underwear of all the males in their household. They also made all their household linens, towels, tablecloths, napkins, and bed linen. The ladies of the hacienda were never idle. To them also fell the task of looking after preservation of food. There were no iceboxes, of course, so milk and cream produced on the ranches were consumed daily. Little cheese was made, and no butter, but milk cooked with sugar was common. It was formed into little shapes to make a confection that could be stored. Fruits could not be canned, for lack of containers, so *ates* became a specialty—fruit pulp boiled with sugar until thick enough to cast into molds, which would keep indefinitely.

People rode about between the haciendas, or took occasional never-to-be-forgotten trips to the nearest town. In general, the *diligencia* was used for journeys. This was a stagecoach with nine or eleven horses spanned in double file behind the lead horse. It was a very skillful man who could manage the complicated reins and control his steeds. To amuse themselves, the hacienda owners (who often owned *diligencias* of their own) sometimes arranged races, and some of those races have become legendary. There is a story of how two *hacendados* with contiguous lands got together and bet on a *diligencia* race, the *diligencias* to be driven by the eldest son of each. The roads were cleared of wandering dogs and pigs; the day for the great race of about thirty miles dawned clear, and the two young drivers sat atop their boxes trying to control their mettlesome horses. Then they were off. The race was run, the *diligencias* did not overturn, there were no casualties. But when the winner stepped down from his box, he found that the tight-pulling reins had stripped the gloves from his hands and the flesh from his fingers.

There is another story of those days of the haciendas which has always moved me. A wealthy *hacendado* married a beautiful young bride, of whom he was inordinately jealous. Though she begged him to arrange some parties, to invite guests, to dispense some hospitality, he never would, for he wished to keep her beauty hidden from the world, to delight his eyes alone.

Then one day all the neighbors for many miles around received invitations for a great fiesta at the hacienda. On horseback, in velvet suits with silver buttons, they began to arrive; the ladies came in carriages, taking care with their many-flounced silk dresses. They were all received by the *hacendado* and attended to their rooms with exquisite courtesy. Trays were sent to them, with word that the great feast would take place next day, after mass in the chapel. The *hacendado's* lovely wife sent her best greetings; she was indisposed.

Next day, somewhat startled, the guests arrived at the chapel for mass. The priest wore black brocade robes, and from the rooms of the *hacendado's* wife came six men, dressed in black, carrying her coffin. It was a mass for the dead, *cuerpo presente*. The poor little wife was given her great fiesta only upon her death.

However, the wealth and the political independence of the great *hacendados* were based to a large degree on privilege and on the labor of others. Their peons, or workers, were really slaves, not in name but in fact, for they could not leave the haciendas where they owed money, nor could they expect to find work at the hacienda of any other landholder, as the *hacendados* naturally stood together. Besides underpaying their workers and keeping them in debt and frightened of leaving, the *hacendados* also dispensed justice very harshly. There was no court save the *hacendado* when the peon got drunk and killed a companion, or ran away, or in some other way infringed on the laws of the state or of the hacienda.

And, meanwhile, the Church had become a great landholder, too. Around the middle of the nineteenth century the Church held a large percentage of the lands of Mexico, most of them rich agricultural fields that were eyed hungrily by landless peasants. When the government also began to think of what these lands might yield in taxes and in produce for the nation, a limitation was placed on the

Church's holdings. A new president had been elected, a little Indian lawyer from the state of Oaxaca, Benito Juárez by name. One of his first acts was to promulgate the Reform Laws, which deprived the Church of its property and, in fact, prohibited it from owning land (though the laws did not expropriate the temples themselves, or otherwise oppress the priests and the religion).

Many of the wealthy people saw the handwriting on the wall and began to fear for their fortunes and privileges. The Church had at all times been a staunch defender of conservatism and, to a large degree, of the special privileges of the wealthy, since they in turn supported the Church. Therefore, the imposition of a foreign emperor on a throne in Mexico was resented only by the rebellious patriots, while the conservatives welcomed the idea, since it was supported by the clergy. At that time the idea of a monarchy still seemed safe and sound to the conservative sector.

Thus it was that when Napoleon III had been persuaded to back the monarchy of Maximilian with French arms, the conservatives and the wealthy and the Church in Mexico were delighted to receive the new court. Maximilian, it seems, was a well-meaning young man who had been deceived into thinking that the Mexican "people" wanted him. It was true that some did, but many others did not. Juárez, who had been elected president, never relinquished his position, even though, as the fight against the imposed monarchy built up, he had to conduct his business as president from inside a modest black coach that carried him away to the north of Mexico.

French arms were defeated on the fifth of May, 1867, in

Puebla, and though the French later retook some lost ground and tasted victories themselves, this was the beginning of the end of the imposed monarchy. The date is celebrated to this day in Mexico with great rejoicing. Foreign countries that occasionally play with the idea of "taking over" Mexico should reflect on the fervor of the Mexican popular celebration of May 5, when the hated foreign government was given its notice to get out.

Things were uneasy in Mexico for a time after the French were expelled; then, in 1876, General Porfirio Díaz entered Mexico City and was proclaimed provisional president.

There followed a long era of peace and of development for Mexico. Even though it is now unpopular to admire Porfirio Díaz, because of his constant re-election and because his regime deteriorated into a genuine dictatorship as years went on, nevertheless credit must be given where credit is due.

Because of Mexico's long history of chaotic unrest, she had never enjoyed any development through investment of outside capital. But under Díaz, who kept order firmly under the military, a great amount of foreign capital, much of it American, came into the country by way of contracts awarding rights and protection for one hundred years or more. Indeed, if Díaz had not guaranteed such protection, it is doubtful that he would have been able to persuade any business to invest in Mexico. But he knew that Mexico had to have electrical companies, railways, other public services, and industry, and this was his way of luring investors.

Mexico began to prosper at last—even though some

mutterings began to be heard, for Americans and Canadians operated the mines, the trolley cars, some railways, and electrical power companies. Americans began to develop the oil and mining; Germans moved in and exploited coffee plantations and hardware businesses; Spaniards began emigrating and setting up chains of bakeries and other stores; French department stores brought in fine goods from Paris.

But Mexico was peaceful, and a measure of native culture began to come timidly into bloom again.

In the provinces many Mexican poets emerged, some of them of authentic quality, and in well-to-do homes there were "salons," and reading circles. The many splendid provincial theaters found that Spanish *zarzuela* companies could be booked on tours. Opera found its enthusiastic patrons, and a Mexican opera company, featuring the legendary Mexican singer, Angela Peralta, competed with groups from La Scala. Caruso sang in the great bullring in Mexico City, and Anna Pavlova danced.

Uprisings of starving and miserable Indians were put down with cruelty. Indians were not allowed in the public parks, and any caught in the streets were summarily carried off to public baths, and their heads were shaved. This was a primitive hygienic measure, as typhus and typhoid were endemic, but it was a humiliating experience. From the head-shaving came the epithet *pelado,* or "peeled one," which distinguished the poor and defenseless from the comfortably well-to-do.

As Porfirio Díaz grew older, his clutch on the country did not diminish, but his powers of judgment did. A host of sycophants surrounded him, and privilege and arrogance became insupportable. In his old age, too, Díaz yielded to the deeply pious feelings of his young wife, and the Church again took unto itself many powers. These were strongly resented by a growing class of young rebels who were almost fanatically anti-clerical.

Eventually the situation came to a boil, and the great Mexican Revolution of 1910 (which lasted many years) was the result.

But of that chaotic and prophetic time we will speak more fully in a later chapter.

8

The Mexican people.

It is not easy to characterize a people. Yet perhaps it is possible to give the visitor, or the tourist in transit, a sketch that may help orient him to certain peculiarities of the people in whose country he is sojourning.

Human nature is the same everywhere in the world, say the sociologists and philosophers. True. But tradition is different, and over the years it exerts different pressures, causing people to behave in different ways.

It must always be remembered that the basic Mexican race is composed of a mixture of Spaniard and Indian. In many sections of Mexico the Spanish blood has contributed little besides the name, and perhaps a few drops of European blood from some generations back. Yet it would be a mistake to think of the people who *look* Indian as being entirely Indian in ideas and behavior. They are Mexicans, too, in their energetic progress toward a better life.

There are small enclaves of pure Indians who have never taken over the Spanish language, or any European ways. Some of them are dying out—for example, the Lacandons, who have been so removed from civilization that they run for their lives when they hear a European coughing, because a common cold can prove fatal to them.

The Tarahumaras inhabit the wild mountains of Chihuahua and a few other northern states. These people are in need of many of the amenities of civilization: general hygiene, an improved source of food, education, and genuine integration into the state that is their native country. Much good is being done in religious and secular missions for these people, and in many other small sections where an almost pure Indian race has for one reason or another been left to one side while civilization rushed past them and forward. Some of these missions are maintained by the Mexican government, others by Mexican- and American-supported private charities and religious institutions.

The Mexican people as a whole are keeping up with what goes on in the world, and tremendous efforts are being made to assure that all can read and write. Illiteracy is being combated steadily. It should not be supposed, however, that the *extent* of schooling really has much to do with intelligence. It has to do with preparation for a certain place in society and in the professions, but there are many Mexicans who, although they have had only a few years of school, are wise, intelligent, and progressive, because their twin weapons—knowledge of how to read and write—have been added to an intelligence already gifted in the arithmetic of daily life, and to a character that centuries of hardship have both toughened and mellowed.

This should be kept in mind, for the simple Mexicans of the countryside—and to some degree the Mexicans of the poorer sections of the city, the servant class and manual workers—have exquisite manners, and a breach of courtesy is to them the immediate sign of poor breeding.

All Mexican men should be addressed as *Señor*, "Sir." Only if one is admitted to friendly familiarity may one use the given name, or the slightly formal prefix *Don*, which used to be a Spanish title of the higher class but which in Mexico is simply one of respect.

Mexicans are protective of their women, and even those who are poor expect courteous treatment of their women and young girl-children. The social pattern brought into Mexico by the Spaniards—by which a home is a fortress and a family's honor is to be defended—persists through every class, for the wealthy inherited the pattern and the middle and poorer classes imitated it.

I may be challenged by many people who have read scientific studies of some selected families from Mexico's poorest, but exceptions prove the rule, even in this. Many of Mexico's truly poor and abandoned people are really up-rooted people, families who have lost their lands or homes and have migrated to the large cities hoping for work. Unprotected by unions, they have fallen into distress and amorality. But something is being done for the country people now. Attempts are being made to help them get employment or return to the land. The problem is a severe one, not likely to be solved in a hurry.

Mexico has an active motion-picture industry. Most of

the films made in Mexico for Mexicans and with Mexican actors show more or less how people live, how they would like to live, and the morals and traditions upon which they base their judgments. To judge by Mexican films, it is obvious that Mexicans still believe strongly in defending the honor of their women, in the Virgin of Guadalupe, in the ideal image of men as great horsemen and impetuous lovers and courteous foes, and in Mexico for the Mexicans. The films still idealize country life and the virtuous country girl, they still portray proudly the accomplishments of the Revolution, and they embody a rich vein of humor, which is often directed at themselves. There are films about modern youth a go-go, pop singers and rock, but underneath, the pattern is still the same.

It will be observed by a student of these films that two characters who are so often the ideal heroine in American films and plays almost never appear in the Mexican ones. These are the dedicated career girl and the sophisticated woman of the world.

Mexican young women are appearing, in large cities, as secretaries, and they train to be teachers and laboratory technicians, and a small percentage try for the stage or the movies, but the career girl, who would turn down an acceptable suitor and marriage for pursuit of her intellectual ambition, is unknown—or rather, she is known about, but is thought to be, quite simply, mad. The sophisticated woman of the world, living as she chooses, taking love where she finds it, and remaining the darling of society, is also an anachronism. Such ladies are immediately classified in Mexico, and they are not heroines. They are villainesses.

Indeed, the American girl's ideal of having her own

apartment, away from the family, is not realized in Mexico. There may be girls who dream of this, but it is simply not permitted. Mexican girls live at home, or with relatives. And they stop work when they marry. Some, it is true, have to go back to work, in the event of a husband's illness or death, but this is necessity, not choice. Careers are not considered to be the ultimate accomplishment.

Mexican widows are rather different from American widows, too. Here is underlined another fact of the Mexican social system. If a Mexican widow must work, she does so. If she has children in their teens, however, probably she will not be allowed to; the children will work and take care of *mamacita*. The American widow frequently works to send her children through college. Higher education is not considered essential in Mexico, and even young men who wish some professional training can get it at night or at odd hours. What would seem unthinkable to the children of a Mexican widow would be to let *mamacita* go out into the world to fend for them.

On the other hand, young men in Mexico are becoming increasingly ambitious to better themselves, and the old Spanish idea of "the dishonor of having to work" has almost entirely disappeared, although there are still some people who hope to "live on their rents." Mexico's general industrial and sociological progress, the laws fixing minimum salaries, and the rising power of labor unions have dignified work. While nearly all Mexicans play the lottery (a state-controlled monopoly) and hope to get rich quick, they are willing to work as well.

It has long been an accepted fact among sociologists that Mexican women are a strong and loyal group. Dr. Enelda

Fox, working for the government as a sociologist, studied all the statistics on abandoned families and found that the percentage of children in Mexico who have been abandoned by both parents is remarkably low. The number of abandoned wives and mothers, however, is very high. Dr. Fox set out to find the reason for this, and came to the conclusion that the Mexican male, if poor and humble, avoids marriage simply because the ceremonies cost so much. By ceremonies he counts the bride's clothes, the licenses, the church wedding, and the feast to follow. So Dr. Fox arranged some fine government-financed fiestas, with music, plenty of good food, and diversion, to follow "multiple weddings," where dozens, at times hundreds, of couples could regularize their status. It proved to be very successful.

While a few small homeless children are occasionally to be seen sleeping in the streets of Mexico City, the government regularly collects them and sees that they have care. There are few orphanages for the simple reason that the Mexican people love children, and simply accept them into their homes, if accidents or death have left children alone in the world. Population statistics very often list *arrimados*, which means "people who live in the same house." These *arrimados* are generally children who are distant relatives or friends of friends.

Here we must not overlook the force of the religious and social role of the *compadres*, the godparents. Upon a child's baptism, the adult who stands sponsor for the child becomes the *compadre*—that is, co-father or co-mother. He is obligated to see that the child is protected and educated if anything should prevent the parents from doing so.

103

Actually the vow he makes applies only to the child's religious and moral training, but the obligation is taken quite seriously, and *compadres* and *comadres* feel a bond closer than friendship, amounting to blood relationship. As a result, the adoption of children is almost unheard of in Mexico. Orphaned children are simply taken home and made a part of the *compadre's* family. And everybody is happy.

So strong is this pattern, the love of Mexicans for children, and the insistence on the necessity of children in the home, that occasionally there is a child robbery, not for ransom, but because some childless woman was simply miserable without a child in her arms.

The position of old people bears out the strong Mexican ideas of family life. As pointed out earlier, families long not so much for education and material betterment as for the warmth and comfort of home, of persons of many differing ages clustered together, sharing, chatting, loving, and living together.

Examples I snatch from my own observation: a woman working as a cook grows old in service, sending all her earnings to her family. She gets through each week doggedly, working loyally and steadily, but the weekend is her paradise, for then her family comes to visit her. I am speaking of my cook, who has been with me for twenty years.

Another example, this time from a very high echelon, as far as family and wealth and distinction go. A friend of mine, a distinguished musician whose career was opening widely to European and American recognition, gave it all up when deaths in the family left him, as the only male, with the "duty" of looking after the estate for his sisters.

Since there are such strong family feelings at every level, it is obvious that convalescent homes and old people's homes, where older members of the family are urged to go and live so as not to burden the younger relatives, are non-existent in Mexico. There is always a home to take in elderly relatives, who are made to feel welcome and loved. In all Mexico there are fewer than ten "homes" for the elderly, and the retirement villages and other such developments for older persons are almost all populated exclusively by foreigners.

Large families, plus the Mexican family feeling, have made this attitude possible and practical. With the advent of more and more industrialization, of apartment-house living, and of limitations of families through planning, the pattern may change. However, so far it has remained constant, and love and respect for older men and women seem a deep part of the Mexican character. To this day, many middle-aged successful men kiss their father's hand on visiting him, and on departing. President Gustavo Díaz Ordaz did just that in the televised report of his first visit home to his elderly parents after being elected.

And *mamacita* is still one of the most powerful words in Mexico. It holds within its affectionate diminutive all the love and respect Mexicans accord their mothers. Mother's Day, a commercial invention often somewhat belittled in the United States, is celebrated with ardor in Mexico.

Another word that expresses all the tenderness of Mexico is *pobrecito* or *pobrecita*. Literally this means "poor little thing," but it carries overtones of warm compassion, and of affectionate concern.

Mexican morals are very strict on paper and in theory, but transgressors are generally pardoned with a *pobrecito* or *pobrecita* on the part of the public. Mexicans have been poor and have starved, so they accept thieves with a shrug of the shoulders and a *pobrecito*. They have endured jealousy and have lived through times of hatred and violence, so they tend not to be vindictive. The Mexican law imposes no capital punishment (save in a few states), and prison sentences for murder are seldom more than twenty years.

On the other hand, it cannot be said, in all truth, that the Mexicans overvalue their lives or life itself. They are devoted to such dangerous and risky spectacles as bullfighting, fast automobile-racing, and sundry dangerous sports.

A popular song goes:

> On the road to Guanajuato,
> Life is worth nothing . . .

And an old revolutionary refrain went, "If they are going to kill me tomorrow, why not now, right away?"

Mexican historical photographs show countless undaunted rebels standing up to be shot, without a quiver of the eyelash to indicate cowardice, or regret at leaving this "vale of tears."

It follows that, thinking little of life, and being inured to much pain and drudgery through the centuries, Mexicans are conspicuously lacking in the Anglo-Saxon fondness for animals, and for household pets in particular.

Due to the general character of Mexican life for the last two centuries—the haciendas, then the chaos of the Revolution, and now the increasing industrialization, which inevitably clusters people into small apartment dwellings near their work—animals have not been semi-personalized, as they have been in our country.

We tend to make pets into personages and endow them with personalities. Everybody knows the feelings (assumed to be general) of a boy for his dog, a girl for her cat, a Westerner for his horse. In Mexico, animals are appreciated in direct ratio to their usefulness. The horse was simply a part of a man's life; the Spanish word for gentleman means "horseman." In the countryside a horse was a working partner; in the Revolution, men fought on horseback.

In the towns, dogs were the policemen, the guards and defenders of each household. This is true even today, because the Spanish principle of "each home a fortress" is still adhered to. There are no roving city police, or certainly not as many as would be needed if householders didn't keep strong, determined dogs and loaded guns in their homes. And cats are respected for their function of keeping down mice. Some families have pets, but the only living creature that seems to be loved and cared for "just because," with no duties to perform to justify his food, is the bird.

Mexicans love songbirds, and even the poorest houses cherish them. Parrots, of course, are doubly appreciated. They can serve as defenders of the home, for they give immediate notice of intruders, as a dog does, but also they are amusing and affectionate. Countless are the Mexican jokes and anecdotes about parrots, and indeed their capacity for loyalty, for long memories, and for intelligence have gone into the folklore.

There was a parrot in Monterrey that bought loads of wood, vegetables, and fruits from passing street vendors, to the embarrassment of his owner, whose voice he imitated perfectly.

There was another parrot who saved a girl from incarceration for life in a mental hospital and regained her inheritance for her. This story may be apocryphal, but it has wide credence in Mexico.

It seems that there was a young woman who was orphaned early and whose inheritance was put into the hands of her *padrino*, or godfather. He had her committed to an asylum and proceeded to enjoy her fortune. But one of the young doctors at the asylum began to believe the girl's story and protestations, and his tests seemed to prove that she was in full control of her faculties. He arranged with hospital authorities to take her home, to confront and accuse her wicked godfather. But the godfather had acted swiftly, and he had bribed all the persons who knew her to assert that she was a stranger having hallucinations.

The girl was in tears, as one after another of her old acquaintances feigned not to know her. However, her parrot remembered her, flew over and perched on her shoulder, and crooned her name. This broke down, first the old nurse, and then the other people; the wicked godfather was confounded, and of course, as in all good stories, there was a happy ending. The heroine regained what was left of her fortune and married the young doctor who had believed in her.

Mexican proverbs and sayings show a great deal about the Mexican character, being full of native wisdom, endurance, and a wry humor. Several sayings about animals illustrate this. "A cock, a woman, and a horse," goes the proverb. "The cock should fill and round out a man's hands, a horse his legs, and a woman his arms." And (this in reference to old men who marry young wives) "For the old cat, a very tender mouse."

The Mexican is extremely sensitive. The reasons for this are probably rooted in his Indian inheritance, for the indigenous peoples were very delicate in their sensibilities. Their poetry is subtle, and their customs and attitudes (despite the outstanding anomaly of the human sacrifice) were gentle and courteous.

To this day, the weapon no Mexican can resist is ridicule. *Quedar en ridículo,* or to be ridiculous, is, for the Mexican, the fate worse than death. Political cartoonists are really feared by politicians, for they have the ability to make the whole country laugh at them, and this is never to be borne.

There is a rather high percentage of suicides in Mexico, especially among children. The pathetic little notes left by these souls who can no longer face a life among their fellows all too often say only that they "were scolded," or feared a scolding, or that they couldn't bear to be made ridiculous.

The note about scoldings is illuminating. Visitors to Mexico constantly note that Mexican children seem extraordinarily well-behaved. A weeping, screaming child being dragged along the street by the hand is seldom Mexican, but more often the progeny of foreigners. Mexicans (though of course there are exceptions, as there are to every generalization) almost never chastise their children in a physical way. They scold or blame, and children are conditioned to think this the most awful of punishments.

Little children customarily are close to their mothers until well out of babyhood. Poor children are carried about with the mother, as she does her work and her errands, in her rebozo; children of more affluent classes always have *brazos*, somebody's arms to hold and cuddle them. In well-to-do families there are nanas or nursemaids, and everywhere there are relatives. Recent studies of psychologists prove what Mexican women have known in their bones for centuries, that babies need constant love, mothering, arms around them, the feel and safety and security of being near someone who loves and cares for them. By the time they reach school age they have a strong fund of security built up in their subconscious. Because of the importance of love and approval, the slightest hint of disapproval is enough to turn almost any mischievous child into an obedient one. Mexican children indeed sometimes burst into tears at a mother's frown. Really obstreperous children are controlled by the maternal pinch. Beatings are simply not administered, and so unusual is any cruelty to children that when occasionally some mentally disturbed person mistreats a child, the incident makes headlines in all Mexican papers.

There are two qualities very much in the Mexican character which are on the negative side. One is the curious preoccupation with what is called *machismo*. This word means masculinity. More than that, it means an aggressive and flaunted masculinity. Many crimes are committed in its name, since so many Mexican men do not understand all the sexual and psychological implications in the image of a man ready to take any physical risk at once, without considering alternatives, and eager to defend any impugnation of his honor, virility, and importance. The person suffering from *machismo* may be a wife-beater, a person who rides a

110

horse to death, a despoiler of virgins, a murderer. He forgives himself anything if the act is meant to display his *machismo* or convince the world of his powerful maleness. It can be seen that this attitude, while dangerous in its extreme form, is also insidious in milder forms. Overindulgence in drink may be a sign of *machismo;* so may an attitude of infidelity in marriage.

Fortunately for Mexico and Mexicans, word is getting about that *machismo* is a kind of illness, and now not so many men are willing to announce themselves as *muy macho.*

Another weakness in the Mexican character is one that, according to some modern writers, is an inheritance from Spain. This is the old sin of envy. Many Mexicans are unable to hear another person praised (unless they do it themselves). Perhaps the emotions of the Revolution, which articulated and justified the resentment of the poor against the rich, have persisted to some degree, for people who have little are bitterly envious of those who have more. The Anglo-Saxon attitude expressed in the phrase, "May the best man win," and the idea of games for the sake of the sport and not for the sake of winning have little acceptance in Mexico. In Mexico one plays to win, one competes with all one's might to be the victor; if one did not want to win, one would not exert oneself at all. This is a practical attitude which actually makes a great deal of sense, whereas the "sporting" ideal is sometimes a rather artificial one. However, this attitude, too, is yielding. The Olympic Games demonstrated to many Mexicans the sheer beauty of competition, without the necessity of being the winner at all times. Now one hears more and more, on Mexican lips, the phrase, *Hay que saber perder,* "One must know how to lose" (gracefully).

Another mild defect is detected in the phrase so often spoken by Mexicans: *Yo no tengo la culpa,* "It's not my fault." Mexicans loathe being blamed, and if they possibly can, they will arrange not to take blame for anything. The servant does not break a dish; the dish "dawned" broken. One does not ruin or spoil a machine; the machine "doesn't want" to go (*no quiere*). Whenever there is trouble, or a crisis, somebody (or maybe several people) cry, *Yo no tengo la culpa!*

Perhaps the outstanding characteristic of Mexicans that impresses foreigners is their attitude toward time. It used to be said that only two things ever began on time in Mexico—mass and the bullfight. So general is this feeling that no Mexican is time's slave that appointments are made "on Mexican time" (arrival anywhere within a couple of hours) or *cita inglesa,* "English time" (arrival within ten minutes of the time agreed upon).

This cavalier attitude toward time is only part of a larger pattern, which can be called "submission to Fate." (Time is definitely part of Fate—the realm of God and angels, out of control of mere man). Mexicans say *Si Dios quiere* about everything, from a possible meeting on a day in the future to a journey or any other plan. "If God wills," it will be accomplished. "God free me," they cry, from any sort of trouble or difficulty. *Dios me libre!* And *Bendito sea Dios* is often on the lips of Mexicans, in heartfelt thanksgiving for some good. "Blessed be God."

Despite a constitution that is aggressively nonreligious, and a governmental stance that is the same, the Mexican

112

people are pious and ejaculations to God are, as they say, "on the flower of their lips" at all times.

A religious marriage is not considered legal, so young people are married *por lo civil,* under the civil law, at home, but they do not live together until after they have gone through the religious ceremony which *blesses* their union.

Even a slowly but steadily growing class of young pragmatists and nonbelievers (growing because the population is growing) conforms to these deeply felt sentiments of the Mexican people.

Their fatalism is linked to their amazing endurance. Their acceptance of God's will is the secret of their patience and of their kindness to the old and unpleasant, and to the young and troublesome.

9

Mexico has produced an astounding number of brilliant and interesting women, whose lives characterize, in some degree, the epochs in which they lived.

I have already spoken of Malintzin, who became Doña Marina following her alliance with Cortes, the Conqueror. She had been a princess in the land near what is now Coatzacoalcos, in the state of Veracruz. Her mother, widowed, had fallen in love with a younger man, who was jealous of her children by her first husband—a circumstance repeated all over the world, in every society, it would seem. The result was that the little princess, Malintzin, was sold into slavery, so that the enamored widow could be free for her lover.

It seems certain that Malintzin fell profoundly in love

with Cortes. With the aid of the Spanish soldier who knew her language, she interpreted for him, and began to teach him other languages. She in turn learned Spanish. Later, when he had tired of her (or when her political usefulness had come to an end), he shunted her off and married her to one of his lieutenants.

Malintzin apparently never rebelled at her fate or betrayed any bitterness or despair. On the contrary, there is evidence that she was a big-souled and gentle woman, for it is told that on an occasion when she accompanied Cortes south to Coatzacoalcos, she met her mother once more. She forgave her, embraced her tenderly, and cared for her from that day forward. No doubt, having learned the power of physical love, she could understand her passionate, erring mother. In any case, Malintzin exemplified filial love and tenderness in her behavior, and so set a pattern that has persisted strongly in Mexico ever since. Mexicans love and respect their parents, care for them when they are old, and make many sacrifices for them. They have not yet succumbed to a blind adulation of and submission to youth, as many other peoples have done.

During the viceregal period another remarkable woman, Mexican-born, came into the world to streak across the horizon like a comet, astounding all who had contact with her. She was Sor Juana Inés de la Cruz, the nun who dedicated herself to studying astronomy, medicine, and painting, to writing, and to a vast correspondence with many brilliant men. One of her famous letters takes issue with a bishop on a matter of theology. He wrote her back, very gently, accepting her point of view but suggesting that a lady of such enormous accomplishments in the intellectual world should devote more time to the cultivation of her immortal soul.

Sor Juana took this greatly to heart. She gathered together all her books and ordered them sold, and the money distributed among the poor. She herself, though somewhat frail, went out into the world to nurse the indigent, who were dying of the plague in Mexico City. She caught it and died in 1695, at the age of forty-five.

The fact that Sor Juana was able to give up all her intellectual and artistic accomplishments to immerse herself in religious and charitable duties also sets a pattern, for the Mexican woman, though as able as any other, has never seemed to be ambitious for acclaim, or to wish to have a career.

While Malintzin and Sor Juana reveal noble traits, there was another lady, of the later viceregal period, who actually saw the end of the Spanish Colony and the emergence of a free Mexico, who had other gifts equally astounding. Her name was María Ignacia Rodríguez, but because she was a blond beauty, and very notorious, the whole country knew her as La Güera (Blondie) Rodríguez. She was of that race of women who are born to be great courtesans, attracting to themselves the most distinguished and brilliant men of their day. She was married three times, each time advantageously, and among her known lovers were the great Simón Bolívar, hero of the Americas; the German scientist, Baron Von Humboldt; and the military adventurer Agustín de Iturbide, who made himself "Emperor of Mexico."

La Güera was probably the only woman who ever appeared before the formidable Inquisition and confounded her judges. It is not known who denounced her, but since "witchcraft" was pursued by the Inquisition, no doubt some jealous rival had accused her of this. It is told that she entered the chamber of the dreaded black-robed judges of the Inquisition dressed in a gown of changeable blue and copper taffeta, with whispering skirts; she wore a black lace mantilla over her shining golden hair, and with a small fan she wafted fragrant small breezes from her perfumed person. She was beautiful, for she had large, intelligent blue eyes, perfect teeth, and a flawless complexion. The last alone was a mark of beauty in those days when smallpox could (and did) ravage the charms of almost everyone. Besides, she had a soft and melodious voice, and she had wit and charm.

Just what she answered the august judges is not known, but it is suspected that she reminded them that just as they judged, they could be held up to judgment. It is not too much to presume that the Güera was not above a little clever blackmail. Anyway, she left the Inquisition chamber leisurely, flirting her fan, and was never summoned again.

What is her place in Mexican history? Well, it appears now, as we study comments that were made on her activities by many of her contemporaries, that she was a sort of Mata Hari, a spy who used her feminine wiles and loveliness to obtain information. The side she was on? It was the side of Independence, for it is known that after Mexico was free of Spain, and Agustín de Iturbide had made himself emperor, he wrote to invite the Güera to be one of his empress's court ladies. The Güera refused, quite sharply. "It was not for the establishment of a monarchy that we worked to be free of Spain," she reminded him.

117

This clever and devious woman, for all her faults, was a true patriot. Mexican women with the same devotion, the same courage, were to emerge in every decade.

We might mention here, in this group of Mexican women, one who was not actually born in Mexico but who became a kind of Mexican symbol. I refer to the little Asiatic who is known in myth and story as La China Poblana. A *china*, in the eighteenth century, was anybody from the mysterious East, hence Chinese. But La China was not Chinese. From all that can be ascertained, she was Hindu, from a port in the south of India. While playing on the beach, she was stolen by Portuguese pirates and sold into slavery. It is said that her name was Myrrha, which means bitterness. While a slave, she took the religion of her captors and became a Christian.

The famous *Manila Galleon*, which twice yearly crossed the Pacific to land in Acapulco with rich cargoes from the Orient and the Philippines, occasionally brought slaves. A merchant from Puebla went to meet the galleon once in order to buy a female slave to care for his ailing wife. He bought Myrrha. The slave girl so sweetly and dutifully cared for the sick woman that her fame spread through Puebla, and thus she became La China Poblana, although her baptismal name was Catarina de San Juan. In her Hindu dress—short-sleeved blouse, full dark skirt, and sari—she went about nursing the sick and poor in the hours she was not needed at the bedside of her patroness. Upon her death there was a concerted effort toward her canonization by the Church, but for some reason this was not carried through. There is no doubt that she was a holy woman, and greatly beloved. Her dress was taken over by the Mexican women, who used their rebozos as she did her sari, and who imitated her dress, though later generations have added rich embroideries to the blouse, spangles to the skirts, and a wide-brimmed Mexican sombrero as a head-dress. Thus it has become the "national costume."

There were many women patriots in the years when Mexico was struggling to free herself from Spain. Josefa Ortiz de Domínguez, the wife of the corregidor (or regent) of Querétaro, was one. At the risk of her life and the lives of her co-conspirators, she sent word to Father Hidalgo, in Dolores, when she heard that the Spanish were about to pounce on many suspected rebels and stifle attempts at independence. To this day, her profile adorns a Mexican coin. The pert Spanish face, with its turned-up nose, is on all copper five-cent pieces. The portrait cannot show a fraction of her courage, her patriotism, and her powers of endurance, for she spent many years in jail.

Far more brilliant, romantic, and exciting (for the only romance attributed to little Josefa is a slightly scandalous imputation that she was in love with her son-in-law, the dashing Ignacio Allende), was the heiress Leona de Vicario. This young lady, an orphan, was of the most aristocratic high society of the early nineteenth century; her enormous fortune was administrated for her by a relative, who thoughtfully arranged for her a proper marriage. But Leona was beautiful, headstrong, and independent. She fell in love with a brilliant young lawyer from the south, who was without money and full of dangerous ideas. His name was Andrés Quintana Roo. Theirs was a flaming love that defied custom, church, and all rules; Leona ran away with her lover and joined in his cause heart and soul. She even went so far as to demand her fortune, so that she might buy cannons for the insurgents, and she figured in an amazing number of captures and escapes. On one occasion her guardian had her incarcerated on the third floor of a convent. But Quintana Roo and several of his friends made a human pyramid, standing upon horses below her window, and passed her down outside the building. As the city gates were closed against her, she did not try to leave the capital at once, but a few days later a little Negro boy, his skin further darkened with coal dust, rode on a pile of charcoal through the gates, unchallenged. He was the intrepid Leona.

Later, as their cause triumphed, and Mexico was freed from Spain, both Leona and Quintana Roo were considered heroes of the Republic. They married and lived happy, respectable lives thereafter.

The Empress Carlota has been the heroine of countless poems and tales, for she was literary material. She was beautiful and doomed; her long lonely years of madness, after the failure of the Empire under Maximilian, are sad to think of. But aside from romantic tragedy, she contributed nothing to Mexico.

Far more truly Mexican, although born of an Italian father, was a contemporary of Carlota about whom less is told. She was Margarita Mazza, daughter of a well-to-do family in Oaxaca. One day the Indian cook of the Mazza family took in and hid a small nephew, a boy who had run away from his home in a nearby village. That boy, illiterate and unprepossessing, years later was to become the husband of the lovely young Margarita. His name was Benito Juárez.

Everyone knows the story of Juárez's stubborn devotion to law, to the Republic, and to the will of the people as expressed in free elections. In Mexico, and in many parts of the world he is revered as a heroic figure. During the years of the French Empire under Maximilian, Juárez insisted on maintaining his position as president of Mexico, though sometimes he was fleeing from French arms, in his simple black carriage, as far north as the American border. But in the end he won and was reinstated. By his side through all the trouble, the uncertainties, and the danger was his wife, Margarita. So profoundly did he trust and love her that Juárez sent her, a timid little Mexican housewife, to speak for his cause in the United States. She grew in stature for the work she was asked to do, and it is reported that after she had addressed the Congress of the United States, pleading the cause of Republican Mexico and her husband, that august body gave her a standing ovation.

When she died, Juárez would allow no one but himself to touch her; he himself laid her in her coffin, kissed the cold forehead, bade her farewell, and closed away forever what had been dearest to him in life.

Around the middle of the nineteenth century there was born in Puebla, daughter of a domestic servant, a girl who was to bring great fame to her native country. She was Angela Peralta. The little girl was short, dark, and stocky, not pretty, but she had a glorious voice, and her mother's employer at once saw that the child had great possibilities. With affection and intelligence, she did everything she could to help Angela. The child sang at parties for some time; then the *patrona* had her properly taught, and at last sent her to Mexico City for final training. A concert was given to raise funds to send Angela to Europe, and like everyone in that day (and to some degree today) she made for La Scala, in Milan. An audition was arranged for her, and around that audition hangs an amusing tale.

The aspirants for places at La Scala sat about, waiting their turns. Angela had not grown handsome; she was undistinguished, dark, and humble, and she was poor. A lovely young Italian singer, dressed in fine silk, had her audition and sang beautifully. Turning to Angela, the only aspirant left, she said, with pride, "That, signorina, is the way we sing in Italy!"

When summoned, Angela came forward to sing. The heavenly voice, full and pure, and of a glowing quality, amazed the judges. When she finished, the leader among them rushed to her, kissed her hand, and announced, "And that, signores, is the way they sing in heaven!"

Angela Peralta achieved enormous fame in Europe; her name became as much associated with the art of singing as did Caruso's, a few years later. But she longed for Mexico. Gathering together operatic troupes, and financing them herself, she gave operas all over Mexico, so that her own people should enjoy what was so deeply appreciated in Europe. She died in Mazatlán, a victim of yellow fever.

Just before the turn of the century, Mexico became enamored of the romantic European idea of literary expression. Poets and essayists congregated together, lovely ladies presided over *salons*, and no doubt there were a good many mutual admiration societies. The astounding thing is that there actually developed in Mexico a large number of fine poets of that era, perhaps because most of them, though influenced by European forms, techniques, and ideas, turned to their own provincial towns and cities and customs for their inspiration.

One of the ladies whose salon was much frequented was a young woman from Saltillo, in the north, a *provinciana*, but a singularly intelligent, beautiful, and exciting personality. Her name was Rosario de la Peña, and almost all the outstanding Mexican poets of her epoch dedicated verses to her. She came to Mexico City later and had a long career as the "muse" and inspiration of many outstanding poets of the day. One poet, Manuel Acuña, committed suicide because of unrequited love for her.

She symbolizes the image of the Mexican woman as an ideal, as an unattainable beauty, cold and distant as a star. This image is seen frequently in Mexican literature, and it went over into drama, and even to some degree into the cinema.

Of another sort entirely is the image of the woman of the Revolution. I do not choose any one of the many women who simply followed their men into the fight, and stayed with them, to feed and look after and comfort them, through all the troubles. There were armies of them, and they constituted, in a very real sense, the commissary.

The Revolution of 1910 was a tremendous upheaval. Men were conscripted on the street, into the federal armies; in the country and in the villages, men rose up behind local leaders and began to engage in guerrilla warfare. On each side the patient Mexican woman, humble and dedicated to her family, followed her man into the war. Often through their spies, the women knew when major battles would take place, and they would contrive to be there, on a nearby hillside, with cooking fires started, when the battle began. They traveled on foot, and often on the tops of troop trains, carrying their little stores of food, their babies, their rifles and blankets. They knew that damp tortillas, kept warm inside their blouses, would generate the green mold that cured septic wounds (primitive penicillin), and they knew that failing mold, damp earth would do the same (primitive Terramycin). They hunted and scrounged for food; they moved into the battles, took their men's rifles, when the men were injured, and kept up the fight.

These women were rough and vulgar and amoral, many of them. But they were brave, resourceful, loyal, and devoted. They did what they felt was their duty and their right—to follow their men and look after them. Babies were born on the march, and buried on the march. The struggle was long and arduous, and because of poor communication, little was known of the outcome at any time. The Revolution became a way of life.

The astounding thing is that these women, the *soldaderas*, did not dress as men or demand masculine privileges. They remained women. They wore skirts, their hair down in braids. And when the dust finally settled and there was peace, they disappeared. They disappeared again into their homes, humble and poor, or middle-class, and once more they took up their lives as wives and mothers in a settled place.

All these women reveal something of the Mexican spirit and of the ideals that still animate the people. Mexican women can be brilliantly intellectual, brave and accomplished, but first and foremost and always, they are wives and mothers, devoted to their homes.

The main plaza in Veracruz, one of Mexico's seaports. The harbor can be seen at the top of the picture

The Street of the Kiss in Guanajuato, so-called because sweethearts need not leave their homes to court; they simply lean over their balconies to kiss

Church in Dolores Hidalgo where on September 10, 1810, Miguel Hidalgo called Mexicans to arms to fight for independence

Left: A French engraving of Maximilian I

Right: Maximilian's wife Carlota, painted in Chapultepec Castle by Albert Graefle

Left: A photograph of Porfirio Díaz, by C. B. Waite

Right: A nineteenth-century engraving of Benito Juárez, from the painting by Chappel

A private hacienda near Guanajuato

The interior patio of a Mexican colonial building, decorated with distinctive, colorful tiles

Two Tarahumara Indians sit at the edge of the Cañon del Cobre in the Sierra Tarahumara of Chihuahua

10

It is a thrilling experience to watch the great Mexican Independence Day parade, which takes place in Mexico City on September 15. One comes away fired with admiration of the splendid Mexican horses, superb animals which are bred from Arab stallions of the purest blood and mares of fine English hunting strains. The result is a mount with the round chest, small head, and magnificent endurance of the Arab steeds, and with the spirit, length of limb, and speed of the English hunters.

It is interesting to reflect how these superb animals came to Mexico. Like the docile little burro, patient beast of burden for the poor of the countryside, the horse was brought to Mexico by the Spanish conquerors. The Spanish horses were of Arab stock, descendants in blood lines from the legendary stallion who was called Drinker of the Wind.

When Cortes, the intrepid, burned his boats behind him at Veracruz, he had with him 508 men, 16 horses and mares, and a colt, which had been born at sea. Perhaps we should say, then, that this colt was the first Mexican horse. Or no. Perhaps the first Mexican horse was that one the Conquerors left with the Itzá Indians, as a gift and in purchase of their friendship. The Itzá Indians worshipped the strange four-footed creature, and on the advice of their priests, lodged it in a splendid house and showered it with attention. They gave it chocolate to drink, and the most delicate rabbits and fishes to eat. They adorned it with plumes and flowers. In their poetic language they gave it a name and made it a god. They called the pitiful creature, slowly dying of hunger among its worshippers, Tzimin-Chac, God of the Thunder. Eventually the weakened legs carried it no more, and the hoofs thundered no longer. Yet Tzimin-Chac remained in the roster of gods for many decades.

The Arab horses of the Conquerors left their strain in Mexico, and some of them escaped and went to live free in the mountains, becoming the wild horses, small and intelligent and wary, that were captured by the roving Indian tribes in North Mexico and in North America. They used them for hunting and war parties. Even today, in remote places, small herds of wild horses roam free.

In Mexico the horse became part of the equipment of a gentleman. Appreciation of the horse was always characteristic of the Spanish. During viceregal days, there were elegant carriage horses for the ladies, and gentlemen rode their spirited mounts. There is an old story told of two carriages which met in a narrow alley in Mexico City. They

126

could not go forward, and they could not go back, for neither passenger would cede the way, thinking the other person one of inferior rank. The story can rouse many emotions, for or against the pride of those carriage owners, who
sat shivering all night, refusing to back up. But no one can
help pitying the horses, enslaved in their owners' egotism,
waiting in their harnesses, hungry, thirsty, and cold.

The horse became part of the great Mexican tradition of
the *charro*, of horsemanship, and of the manly arts. The
horses of the diligences are protagonists of countless stories
of prowess and heroism. The horse is celebrated in great
Mexican ballads, too, such as "On my paint horse," and
"Siete Leguas," which means "Seven Leagues," the name of
Pancho Villa's almost legendary mare.

A colloquy which could be dramatic as well as enlighten-
ing can be imagined between the wonderful "Siete Leguas"
and the "Rayo de Plata," or Silver Streak, which was the
beautiful white horse ridden by that other Mexican folk
hero, Emiliano Zapata. Superstitious souls still claim that
when they see the ghost of Rayo de Plata streaking across
the dark hills of Morelos, trouble is coming. Alas, the
owner of Siete Leguas and the rider of Rayo de Plata were
both assassinated by treachery and in ambush.

Today, on the bridle paths of beautiful Chapultepec
Park in Mexico City, one can see the descendants of all the
historic and dramatic horses of Mexico, pacing genteelly,
carrying proud gentlemen dressed in the garb of the country squires of a hundred years ago.

During the nineteenth century the ranch life of Mexico
was based on horsemanship, and all the arts of the rodeo,
now used so much in the United States for entertainment

and as a spectacle, were developed as a part of the working life of the rancher.

Mexico is one of the few countries that still preserve a cavalry, though that too, it is said, is giving way to mechanization—the tank and the helicopter.

But while the horse in Mexico was identified with the rich and powerful, with gentlemen, with the hacienda life on the great ranches, and later with the amazing heroes of the Revolution, the patient little burro has always been the companion and helper of the poor man. The burro, to many people, symbolizes something very typical of Mexico. This is somewhat sentimental and anachronistic, for Mexico is forging forward into the vanguard of the industrialized nations of Latin America. Yet the burro is still important. Loaded with wood or with green fodder or with vegetables, or dragging two great girders, one lashed to each side of his little body, the burro is still a design on the horizon, a part of every stretch of scenery, a factor in the lives of the people.

The poor Mexican lives on corn. It is shaved off the cob, and dried and pounded into the *masa* for tortillas, the very base of the poor man's food. The burro lives on the corn cobs and whatever grass he can manage to find in his daily life of work.

It was the Conquerors, the soldiers, who brought the horse to Mexico. It was the friars, who came after them, who brought the burro. They knew the donkey to be extremely useful in rural Spain, and they hoped the burro might relieve the Indians of carrying their own burdens. Perhaps the friars also wanted to facilitate their own work of building convents and schools, for which they had to enlist the labor of the Indians. The friars were diligent in trying to Christianize and educate the pagans of New Spain, and they were helped in this gigantic task by the little donkeys they had sent from Spain, which were the progenitors of the race of patient burros in Mexico.

When today one sees a burro overburdened, it is well to remember that the people overburdened themselves, uncomplainingly, not many decades ago.

Surely there is nothing more endearing in the world than a newborn baby burro, all soft fluffy fur and long-lashed, melting eyes. Not many people are aware of the fact that there is a decent trade in young burros; many Americans who come to Mexico as visitors buy them for their children at home. And the favorite figure in all sorts of artifacts for the export trade is the flop-eared little animal, with his tiny black hoofs, his expression of quiet patience, his evident good nature. The burro figure is seen in clay, in carved onyx, in wood, and is the favorite design for piñatas, those paper-decorated jars of sweetmeats that are crashed open at children's parties.

Around the end of the year the burro appears in countless Mexican homes as the *Nacimiento*, or Christmas crêche is set out in the living room, for the donkey is associated with every dramatic moment in the story of the Holy Family. When, in the nine days before Christmas, Mexicans celebrate the *Posadas*, or the "asking for lodging," the pilgrims carry images of the Holy Family, and always a little burro, for tradition says Mary was seated on one when Joseph took her up to Bethlehem for the census. "And there was no room at the inn," as everyone remembers, so the Holy Child was born in the stable, while the innocent beasts looked on with wondering eyes. The stable was warmed by their clover-sweet breath and sanctified by their innocence.

Legend urges us to ponder over the fact that clearly marked on his back, in darker fur, every little burro carries an unmistakable cross.

The association of the burro with all that is humble has never faltered, down through the ages, and much of the idealization of Mexico's enduring and uncomplaining poor may come from their association with the *burrito*.

Visitors to Mexico, especially if they are Anglo-Saxon, are often distressed to observe that there are many street dogs, apparently homeless, some of them ill and starving. The dogs are allowed to run freely, to breed as they will, and to forage for themselves.

For a partial understanding of the situation, we must take a look at history. When the Spaniards arrived, they found that the native peoples had four types of domesticated dogs.

One type was a dog commonly used for food, the flesh of which was said to be of good flavor. The animal (comparable to the Chinese "chow" dog, which was also raised as a food animal) was a distinct type that has completely disappeared, and for a curious reason. It is told that the Spaniards themselves, traditional meat-eaters, took aboard great numbers of these dogs to serve as food on their voyages back and forth across the Atlantic, for they were easier to care for than cattle or sheep. So completely did they follow the custom of eating these little creatures that the breed has completely disappeared.

Another type of dog was exterminated by the Spaniards

deliberately. This was a fierce and strong dog which individual Mexican families kept for their personal defense. The dogs were first prohibited and then simply wiped out.

A third type of canine, said to be hump-backed, existed and had been to a large degree domesticated when the Spaniards arrived. For some reason not known, this dog also has disappeared.

All the above types of dog and one other were described in detail by the first Spaniards. They did not tell about the little Chihuahua dog of the north, for they had not yet gone far enough into the northern mountains to find it, and the dog, swift and small, customarily lived in burrows.

The last type, called the *esquintle*, was a household pet and much loved. Children were called *esquintles* as tribute to the playfulness and affection and endearing qualities of the dogs. In pre-Conquest times the *esquintle* was often buried with his master, so that the dead person would have his companionship and love along the lonely ways of the afterlife.

This little dog—small, plump, and hairless—is still seen today, bred for dog shows, but at the time when the Spaniards arrived, it was very sturdy and it reproduced freely. It is told that in Mexican homes the *esquintle*, which although hairless is very hot-blooded, was used as a sort of living hot-water bottle, often sleeping at the feet of the master and the children to keep them warm. Old people were always given an *esquintle* to cuddle, to keep old bones warm and to comfort their rheumatism with the little hot, throbbing bodies.

The *esquintle* was allowed to run about freely, as were all the other dogs. (There was no traffic to be a danger to them, and there is no record that rabies was known in that time.) This is a Mexican tradition; in small villages chickens are permitted to run about and forage, and so are the pigs.

A remnant of this feeling persists, for the poor all have dogs, and, in their tradition, allow them to roam about and to get their food as best they may. However, as can be seen, this custom causes difficulty today, and the Mexican government is now careful to conduct regular campaigns to collect and eliminate homeless dogs in order to protect them and the people from rabies, which is a problem, especially in states where there is a hot dry summer. Owners may take dogs to be examined for rabies and injected free, and people who have been bitten by dogs or other animals supposed to be rabid are given the series of shots gratis by the health department.

In this connection it is interesting to note that the Mexican government has conducted a great number of campaigns to wipe out diseases that have been endemic for centuries and to clear the country of smallpox and malaria. The government is also trying to protect cattle against hoof and mouth disease, and hogs against cholera.

With reference once more to dogs and small animals, in most of the Mexican cities of any size there are now humane societies, which house homeless animals, try to place them, and when necessary, put sick or injured creatures painlessly to sleep.

Mexicans love birds, and few homes are without caged *censontlis* (nightingales), larks, or canaries. But the favorite is still the mysterious and amusing parrot. Some poetic Mexican writers have referred to the flocks of parrots that live in tropical forests as "green clouds." It is certain that the parrot is sought after as a pet, and indeed, Mexicans rely on parrots to give notice of intruders, as we rely on dogs.

There is a difference of opinion about how to choose a parrot. Some say he should have a black tongue; others say he must have a touch of gold in his head feathers. To see baby parrots, not yet fully feathered out, sitting unhappily in their little cages, awaiting customers who will choose them, is touching. But there can be little pity for the parrot once he has been taken home to become the petted darling of the mistress of the house or of the cook. Fed on bananas and on bread soaked in coffee, fruits, and other dainties, he grows fat, pleasant, and affectionate, and becomes a choice conversationalist. Though there are people who insist that parrots think, this may be disputed, but they certainly are good company, in spite of their non sequiturs.

I knew a parrot who regularly sang all the trumpet calls of the Mexican army; he had passed his tender youth in a barracks. Another piously prayed his rosary every evening as soon as it began to get dark.

If anyone wishes to do deep psychological research on the Mexican character, I recommend that he study Mexican parrots, what their owners teach them to say, and the thousands of jokes about parrots and in which parrots figure. They all show the curious humor, the sly malice, the compassion, the sharp sense of ridicule, and the mordant wit of the Mexicans.

11

A delightful cartoon portrays two American tourists, recognizable by their costumes and the quantities of cameras hung about their persons, who are shown in a sort of Mexican plaza, surrounded by dozing, straw-hatted Mexicans. One says to the other, "Are you sure they said this was fiesta time?"

Naturally, they had said it was siesta time.

But almost every day is fiesta time somewhere in Mexico. As the Mexicans themselves say, "Every little chapel has its fiesta once a year." The *dicho*, or saying, is to remind people that every cloud has a silver lining, but we may take it literally as well. There is a fiesta for every saint in the calendar, and some of them are very great fiestas indeed. One of them is nationally celebrated. Even the government, so resolutely nonreligious, can't stop the celebration of Guadalupe Day, for Our Lady of Guadalupe is supremely dear to Mexican hearts.

Our Lady of Guadalupe appeared to a simple Indian, spoke to him in Nahuatl, and called him "Little son" and promised to watch over him and his people always. Because of this promise, there is blazoned over the great Basilica of Guadalupe the words, "She did this for no other people."

This is the story:

The year was 1531. Dozens of priests had poured into New Spain with the Conquerors, bringing the Christian faith, education, and the Spanish language to the native peoples. A poor Christian Indian, who had taken the name Juan Diego, was hurrying across a barren hillside from his village home toward the great church that had been built at Tlatelolco. Suddenly, on the hillside of Tepeyac, he heard sweet music, and then he saw a vision. A girl of his own people, dark in color, simply dressed, with dark doe-eyes, came toward him and spoke to him sweetly. She told him that she was called the Virgin, and that he must go and tell the priests to build her a church there.

Juan Diego, though he felt himself too humble for the task of the lady who had appeared to him in a cloud of radiance, did as he was told, and had to go back to Tepeyac to report that the bishop did not believe him, would not listen to him.

Inspired by the Lady, Juan Diego three times visited Bishop Zumárraga with his request, and was denied. However, the bishop said, on the occasion of his last visit, "Bring us some sign that what you say is true." The Lady then provided Juan Diego with a sign. "Open your mantle," she commanded him, and though it was the twelfth of December, a wintry cold day, and no flowers bloomed, she filled his *tilma* with fragrant roses. Juan Diego hurried with this "sign" to the bishop, and behold, when he opened his cloak, letting fall the lovely roses, which perfumed the whole room, there appeared on it the image of the Lady, the Virgin, who had used him for her messenger.

As everyone knows, the basilica was built, and countless miracles are attributed to the intercession of the Lady Coatashupe, Our Lady of Guadalupe.

So profoundly did the Mexican people identify their interests with the Virgin of Guadalupe that she appeared on the banners of the first insurgents who tried to break free from Spain in 1810. The Spaniards thereupon elevated an image of Our Lady of the Remedies (Nuestra Señora de los Remedios), who was honored in a great church just outside Mexico City, to the position of general in the Royal Army. Into the fray they carried the foot-high image, dressed in warlike garb. This war soon was called "The War of the Holy Queens," for the two images of the Virgin were carried into battle and were apparently taking sides, one being for Spain and royalty, and the other for the insurgents who wanted to be free. When the insurgents won, and Mexico did, in effect, become free, a solemn ceremony was performed in which the Virgin of the Remedies "surrendered." She was forced to give up her uniform as a general, and to promise never again to take up arms.

Our Lady of Guadalupe has played many strange roles since the day she was carried into battle by the insurgents. During the Revolution, in 1910, the followers of Zapata, in

Morelos, wore her image sewed to their big straw sombreros.

And she has been censored. The original words of Padre Hidalgo, when he rang the bells at Dolores and called upon Mexicans to fight to free themselves from Spain, were: "Long live Our Lady of Guadalupe! Long live Mexico, and death to bad government!" Every year when the president of Mexico reiterates the "Grito" or Cry of Dolores, he exclaims, "Long live Independence! Long live Mexico! Long live Mexico!" Our Lady of Guadalupe is not mentioned.

Nevertheless, the country has thousands of Lupes and Lupitas, named for the beloved image of Our Lady. The twelfth of December, her feast day, is a national festival and, to Catholics in Mexico, a holy day of obligation when they are required to attend mass. In every city and town in the country there is a church of Guadalupe; in larger cities there are many. In 1824 the first constitutional president, Félix Fernández, called himself Guadalupe Victoria, in honor of the most Mexican of apparitions of the Virgin, and of victory over the Spanish.

The original mantle of Juan Diego, on which appeared the portrait of Our Lady of Guadalupe, is on display over the high altar in the great Basilica of Guadalupe, to which come pilgrims from all over Mexico, to render homage, to make promises, to give thanks. On the eve of August 15, the Assumption of Our Lady, the people of a village in the Puebla hills come down and spend all the night making a great carpet of flowers on the floor of the basilica, so that next morning "it dawns" beautiful and fragrant as an offering for the beloved Virgin.

All through the year different cities and sections of Mexico have dates set aside for them to visit the Basilica of Our Lady of Guadalupe. Some come in pilgrimages, walking for many days, as do the people of Querétaro and some other towns. Many come in bus loads, and train loads, from Monterrey, Guadalajara, Campeche—from everywhere. And on certain specified days different professions and interests join to make their pilgrimage to the Virgin—the Japanese colony in colorful kimonos, the actors and musicians, the Chinese residents, the chauffeurs and taxi drivers, the lawyers, the doctors, and so on and so on.

An interesting story is told of the power of Our Lady of Guadalupe to protect her own. At one time numerous Chinese came to Mexico, and while there, many of them married Mexican wives. Later on, having prospered, many of these families returned to China. During the invasion of China by Japan, there was great turmoil, and numbers of these women, who were Mexican citizens still, wished to return to Mexico. In the chaos, however, and in their headlong retreats before the invading armies, many of them were without papers. Mexican consuls were instructed to assume Mexican citizenship on the part of each one who could produce a little image or medal of the Virgin of Guadalupe. And so dozens were rescued.

Of course, while the great fiesta is Guadalupe Day, December 12, there are many other feast days of great splendor and devotion. Most of them, of course, are connected in some way with the Catholic faith and its long list of saints, and many are days of special devotion because of some connection with the Holy Family. The Day of Our Lady of Carmen, for instance, is observed on July 16, and coincides with what was formerly a great harvest festival in the states to the south of Mexico City. On this day there is a brilliant fiesta called the Guelaguetza, with native dancing, in the state of Oaxaca, near the capital city. Every little (or large) church dedicated to Our Lady of Carmen celebrates a fiesta on July 16, and many have native dancers, called Matachines, performing all day in the church gardens. Then there is December 8, the day of the Immaculate Conception. The Conqueror Cortes was much devoted to this feast day, and himself ordered several churches dedicated to the Immaculate Conception. All the Conchas in Mexico are honored on December 8. And there are other great days, such as Corpus Christi, which also honors everyone named Manuel or Manuela, and which for some reason is celebrated by many children, dressed as little Indians in native costume, and often carrying miniature birdcages, small laden burros, and so on.

The fiestas, besides featuring native dancers and music, always provide the special Mexican dishes that are the delight of the people. Although *ho-cakes, ho-dogs* (or even in literal translation *"perros calientes"*), *beesquits,* and other American delicacies have been taken up enthusiastically by the Mexicans, whenever a man or woman celebrates his saint's day the feasts are more likely to feature the rich and wonderful Mexican cuisine.

There is no doubt that the Mexican kitchen has given the world treasures to be remembered. One of the most delicious begins with chocolate, native to Mexico, which is ground, mixed with sugar, almonds, and vanilla or cinnamon, and is molded into tablets or bars. These can be dissolved in milk, heated, and finally beaten to an iridescent foam. This is Mexican chocolate, a drink that became so popular even in the early days of the Colony that the bish-ops had to prohibit the congregation from bringing hot brimming cups to mass, because the people put all their attention on the delicious drink and not on their spiritual duties.

The Mexican tortilla—corn kernels dried, then slaked in a mild lime solution, ground to a paste, and finally patted into a very thin cake which is baked quickly on a hot sheet of metal (*a comal*)—is the basis of an endless variety of toothsome dishes. Mexicans use tortillas as bread; they fill them with tidbits of meat, cheese, tomato, and chili, in an enormous variety of combinations, to make tacos, fried or merely heated and rolled around the filling. When the filled tortilla is covered with a sauce spiced with chili, it is called an enchilada, and again, there are dozens of varieties of enchiladas—green, white, black, red, with cream or with cheese.

Then there are other Mexican specialties. Tamales are ground corn beaten with shortening and seasoning, filled with spicy morsels of meat and sauce, the whole folded into dried corn husks and steamed. These can be prepared as a sweet, too. In Yucatán there are innumerable recipes for the preparation of deer and wild birds; around Veracruz and Campeche, on the coast, flourish varied and subtle tra-ditions for the flavoring of fish and seafood.

But in two other departments of food the Mexican kitchen has taken over the Spanish way with certain staples —bread and sweets. The breads of Mexico are immediately remarkable for tastiness and variety. Many regular visitors to Mexico provide themselves with large plastic sacks, which they take home full of freshly baked *bolillos* and *tel-*

eras (salt rolls). These can be frozen, and taken out for reheating, coming to the table as fragrant and crisp as if they had emerged that moment from their Mexican oven.

When President Kennedy made his state visit to Mexico in 1962, he ordered several hundred *bolillos* bought and stowed in his plane, on his return, so that he could enjoy them in the White House.

Besides the salt rolls, which rival the tortilla as the accompaniment for any meal, Mexicans make a variety of sweet breakfast rolls that are as fanciful as they are delicious. There are *novias*, or "brides," which are little mounds of sweet dough baked and covered with a powdering of white sugar; *nueves*, snail-shaped rolls; braided rolls, rolls flavored with orange-flower water, rolls flavored with anise, rolls sprinkled with toasted sesame seeds, all sorts of butter rolls like croissants (called *cuernos*), and egg rolls of several kinds. There are rolls that have little ears like cats, and others shaped like braided fastenings for a coat; there are rolls with a strip of dough made to look like teeth in a wide smile; there are rolls covered with honey glaze, powdered with nuts, decorated with toasted coconut.

The American breakfast of orange juice and black coffee is looked upon as a severe penance in Mexico, where bread is one of the gifts of the gods.

There are great holidays which call for special breads as well. One of these is the great fiesta of the Day of the Dead. The second of November, celebrated in the Catholic calendar as the day of the Faithful Departed, is observed with colorful piety and with fanatical devotion in Mexico.

The ancient Mexicans, regardless of their language or

origin, all seemed to share a common devotion to the dead, and those racial memories have carried over to adorn and Mexicanize the Day of the Dead. Work comes to a standstill; families stay up all night and keep vigil in the cemeteries over the tombs of their dead; all day visitors arrive at the graveyards, there to picnic and to pass the day—all day —singing and talking, keeping company with the spirits of their departed.

On this day in countless Mexican homes altars are arranged with offerings for the dead—favorite dishes, bread and cake and candy. The candy takes the form of little sugar-skulls, chocolate hearses, or other trappings of burial. In newspapers, obituaries of living persons appear in verse; that is a kind of journalistic homage. Sweethearts give each other fancy sugar-skulls, with their names spelled out in gilt paper. There is an atmosphere of jollity and good humor about most of these traditions. At the same time, of course, many people solemnly attend masses to commemorate their dead.

On November 2, and for a few days before and after the date, a special loaf appears in all the bread shops. It is called Dead Man's Bread, and it is one of the most delicious breakfast breads to be obtained anywhere. The wheat dough is kneaded with sugar and orange-flower water, and formed into round, high loaves, which are then decorated with designs in pulled dough. The loaf is often decorated with red or pink sugar, as well.

On January 6, the Day of the Magi, another wonderful bread is offered in all Mexican bakeries. This is the *rosca de reyes*, a sweet loaf formed into a circle and decorated with candied fruits—cherries, figs, citron, and raisins. This bread always contains a tiny porcelain doll, the Niño Dios, little Child Jesus. In Mexican homes this bread is eaten by families and friends, with thick foaming chocolate. The person who gets the Niño in his portion is obligated to give everyone present a great party on Candlemas Day, the second of February.

The wonderful sweets of Mexico came in with the Spaniards, who had adopted many of them from the more sophisticated Moors. Since many of these sweets are of Arabic origin, it is not strange that they rely heavily for flavor and texture on honey, almonds, dates, and crystallized fruits.

Around Christmas time Mexican candy stores display mouth-watering "covered fruits," *frutas cubiertas*, which are oranges, pears, plums, peaches, and sections of pumpkin that have been simmered in a sugar syrup until crystallized, then carefully dried. There are trays of bananas cured with sugar and pressed into blocks. In Mexico, as in Spain, there are marzipan figurines in every sort of shape and color, as well as almond candies in crisp blocks, or in soft or chewy pieces. Then there are literally dozens of kinds of "burned milk," which means whole rich milk cooked with sugar until stiff enough to form into shapes. These are of great variety, some being combined with such fruits as the guava, and with nuts and cinnamon. And there are thousands of varieties of candies made of coconut. Mexicans have taken up the American "chocolate cream," but it has not displaced the old-time sweets.

In the centuries before the icebox, fruits were preserved by boiling down the pulp with sugar until it became a thick paste, and then casting it into molds. These fruit *ates* are still a favorite on Mexican tables, and are often served with one or another of the great variety of cheeses now produced in the country.

Packaged and frozen foods are now coming into vogue in Mexico, and as the country industrializes and more and more women take factory jobs, there will be fewer servants to dedicate themselves to the day-long tasks of the difficult and exacting Mexican kitchen.

However, it may be expected that gourmets who appreciate the splendor of a good Mexican table (second only to the Chinese in variety and sophistication and poetry) will be able to count on enjoying many of the wonderful old-fashioned Mexican dishes for some decades to come.

12

The Mexicans are an ancient people, very ancient. From the remote past some wonderfully expressive legacies have come down to us in the form of architecture and sculpture.

We have tiny sculptured figurines in clay dating from more than ten centuries before Christ, which show the clothing worn by the people, and many of their activities, not excluding surgical operations. (There are statuettes showing a trepanning, for example, and a few have been found indicating that the ancient peoples practiced the Caesarian operation in difficult births.)

Equally representative of the art of the ancient peoples are the astounding buildings they have left to us, which show us their grasp of the use of decoration, their delicacy in working stone, their mastery of the principles of mass and space. It is amazing to reflect that these edifices, many of which are still standing today, were built without knowledge of the arch, without the wheel or draft animals. Yet the stones forming the buildings have been set together with such art and precision that they are marvels today.

It seems logical to assume, judging from the ancient builders' evident familiarity with acoustics, that they had mastered the basic principle of vibrations, and it has been suggested that they developed a method of raising great weights of stone by a combination of levers and of vibrations caused by the tones emitted by stones struck successively with wooden mallets or with other stones.

The sculpture that has come down to us as decoration on temples or tombs, or on commemorative stellae, as well as carved figures of gods and priests, is evidence of a stylization that was artistically sophisticated. Much of the ancient stone sculpture is somewhat grotesque in its exaggerations of decorative themes or posture, but this was probably consciously sought, for often the gods were demons or were meant to inspire terror and respect.

However, there are tender simplicities in the sculpture too—small animal forms of great appeal: rabbits, turtles, little dogs. And there are many beautifully and delicately carved examples of coiled serpents, which are as meticulously worked from below as from above. (One may see these in Mexican museums, displayed with mirrors, so that one can appreciate the entire sculptured object.) The serpent is a constantly recurring theme.

The ancients were not without painting, too, for many murals have been found in excavations made at Palenque, and in the sites of other pre-Conquest cities.

With the arrival of the Spaniards and the establishment of the viceregal court, painting on canvas came into vogue, and was practiced as in Spain. This developed a great school of painting, for in the sixteenth and seventeenth centuries Spain produced some of the greatest painters the world has known. To this day, at least two of them are called the "painters' painter," which is the highest compliment of any. The great compliment is given to Velázquez (died in 1660) and El Greco (died in 1614). The first Spanish painter to follow Cortes to the New World was Cifuentes, but his work was soon surpassed by the paintings of the Mexicans Cabrera, Echave, Villalpando, and the Juárez brothers, whose subjects were religious themes.

Portraiture seems to have suffered in those early years in Mexico. A display of the portraits of the viceroys, to be seen in one of Mexico's historical museums, shows work singularly stiff and without imagination. Further, all the faces seem harsh, sly, and cunning. Could this have been the case? Not entirely. There were some viceroys of genuine humanitarianism and progressive policies.

Some great paintings were sent to Mexico, by Philip II and his successors, for the adornment of the churches, among them canvases by Tintoretto, Murillo, and Ribera.

Yet the most interesting development in art in Mexico came during the nineteenth century, when the population was scattered about the countryside in large landholdings, in tiny rich cities clustered around silver mines, and in the few large cities where people of wealth were able to hire painters to produce portraits of themselves and their families. A profession of wandering painters came into being whose names are unknown to us. They went from hacienda

147

to hacienda and from town to town, painting portraits. Sometimes they would stay for months on a hacienda, sharing the life of the patron and his family, painting them all, as well as any and all visiting relatives. These portraits are often mere studies of front face or profile, without grace, the colors without subtlety. But it is evident that the painters made every effort to secure a genuine likeness, and for this reason the portraits have a peculiar stiff charm.

Among the paintings from this epoch are many that are very touching. In those days, when there were no photographers, children on the haciendas (and indeed, all over the world) often did not survive childhood illnesses. Then evidently, when a child died, the call went out in urgency to the nearest itinerant painter, asking him to come posthaste with his canvas, brushes, and colors to paint the little dead child, so that the family could have a remembrance of how he looked. But the painters, being on the whole literal-minded, painted exactly what they saw. So we have a whole series of anonymous portraits of little ones, from babyhood to the ages of ten or twelve, painted with pale little dead faces, sad half-closed eyes that will never look upon the world again, pale small mouths still drawn in expressions of pain and bewilderment.

The work is not art in the full sense, but it is a genre that is poignant and impressive. And there is little doubt that here began the Mexican surge toward realism which exploded into the great Mexican renaissance of mural painting in the twentieth century.

Other precursors of the modern muralist movement in Mexico, with its passionate devotion to all things Mexican and to the Mexican people themselves, were the painters who in the nineteenth century began to paint scenes of Mexican life. To them we owe countless canvases—some good, some poor—of Mexican kitchens, of street corners showing little groups of serape-swathed, sombreroed men and hurrying women wound in their rebozos. They painted country scenes of *tientas* or "improvised bullfights," of roping and branding of cattle, of riders on mettlesome mounts.

Another realistic painter of the nineteenth century was the landscape artist, José María Velasco. Here, however, was no journeyman painter, no mere annotator of Mexican tradition and customs. Velasco was a superlative artist, dedicated to his self-imposed task of painting the Valley of Mexico—but the Valley of Mexico in its surrounding of space, of celestially blue skies and golden air. Absolute master of the principles of perspective, with his delicate palette Velasco produced works that are justly considered national treasures.

With the twentieth century there came into being a new school of painting in Mexico which was to startle and later to influence the whole world. Mexico's reputation as the leader in mural painting began with the Revolution, for the struggle of the masses was the theme of the great muralists who dedicated themselves heart and soul to painting the revolutionary message. These were Diego Rivera, José Clemente Orozco, and David Alfaro Siqueiros. These three men were of greatly differing characters and talents, but one who looks at their work as a totality can see how they complemented and harmonized with one another.

Diego Rivera, born in Guanajuato, began drawing and painting as a small child. His mother made many sacrifices to send him to study in Europe, where he dutifully copied masterpieces and traveled about, thinking and practicing. When he returned to Mexico, already imbued with the revolutionary spirit, he allied himself with the burgeoning movement in Mexico. The triumphant revolutionary government gave him walls to paint on, and his art began to flower. Since he already knew the classical techniques of his art—composition, color harmonies, and rhythms—and was an excellent draftsman, Diego was prepared to focus his attention on representing his ideas. He painted great murals in the National Education Building, in Chapingo at the National Agriculture School, in the Palace of Cortes in Cuernavaca, and in the National Palace in Mexico City. His earliest works, revealing much poetry and deep feeling, began to give way to later work in which techniques were even more certain but in which his themes became almost pure propaganda, praising the machine, the overalled worker, the gods of the Russian Revolution, and similar idols. Diego's work in Mexico naturally idealized the humble and patient Indian of the countryside, and in general he revealed himself an implacable enemy of the Church, of capitalists, and of the Spanish Conquerors. In a later mural, in the National Palace, he even went so far as to portray Cortes as a hunchbacked syphilitic. During his lifetime one or two of his paintings were rejected in the United States, but in his own country he enjoyed enormous prestige and power.

Diego was very much a child of our century; among other things, he knew the value of publicity. Being extremely clever and astute, he managed to appear in headlines in Spanish and in English with great regularity, and he became known all over the world, not only as an out-standing artist but as a unique and arresting personality. Tall, heavy-set, with a blunt-featured, broad face lit by prominent, satirical, and piercingly intelligent dark eyes, he customarily dressed himself in workman's garb—suits of blue overalls, with a red bandana around his neck and a broad-brimmed felt hat. He was unmistakable and unfor-gettable, two qualities of enormous value for a man who feels he has an important message to impart. Diego used his canvases and his walls for this message.

His easel painting showed his domination of many tech-niques, and he was in great demand as a portraitist, but his greatest work, in which he had the most heartfelt interest, was the murals. He was a prodigious worker and left be-hind him a great body of painting. Unfortunately, some of it has been deteriorating seriously because of the effects of the weather, or possibly because modern paints are not as durable as the ones used in ancient times by mural painters. Attempts have been made to restore Rivera's murals, but these are not always satisfactory.

One of his most charming murals is a large one painted for the Hotel Prado, which depicts a Sunday afternoon in the Alameda Park—a work that recalls Sunday prome-nades from Diego's youth. Diego, painted as a boy, is shown holding hands on the one side with his third wife, Frida Kahlo, and on the other with a skull-death image. The whole is suffused with a springtime, sunlit atmosphere of great beauty. Many historical personages are represented in the background, including an atheistic thinker Diego admired, who displayed a pennant reading "There is no God." This brought on an earth-shaking scandal, for the hotel owners had invited Mexico's Archbishop Luis Martínez to bless the mural at its unveiling. Robed and ready to carry out the rite, Monsignor Martínez caught sight of the small irreligious pennant in the midst of the great painting, and refused to bless it.

Catholic students tried to deface the mural; defenders of artistic freedom fought them. In the end, the hotel was obliged to cover up the wall for some years. At last they brought the painting out again, and visitors may now see it in the main lobby. The phrase on the offending pennant has been thoughtfully changed to one that arouses no passions.

José Clemente Orozco, a native of Jalisco, was also fired with revolutionary spirit. His work is thought by many critics to have greater impact than Diego's, while possibly it is less incredibly perfect as to draftsmanship. In fact, a posthumous story is told that Frida Kahlo, herself an excellent painter of easel work, once said: "Diego is an enormous talent without genius, whereas Orozco is an enormous genius without talent."

The fact is that Orozco's work is passionate and powerful, and sometimes grotesque. His later murals were often done in gray, white, and ochre, the artist eliminating every detail from the original design in work that seems powerfully direct and strong.

Like Diego, he was commissioned to work in the United States at various times, but the bulk of his finest painting is to be seen in Mexico: in Mexico City and in Guadalajara.

A story is told of Orozco that once at a banquet a guest was impertinently asked if he had not said that Orozco's work made him literally sick. The discomforted guest, in Orozco's presence, had to admit that he had indeed said so.

"I meant, and I mean," he explained, "that your work moves me so that I cannot bear it. It makes me literally ill."

"Certainly," agreed Orozco. "That's why I paint."

Queried about his custom of drawing directly on the wall, without laying out the design in carefully transferred squares of drawing, he answered that that was how he worked. "Once the design is worked out on paper, and I have it in my head, I go right at the wall," he answered.

"But," stammered the reporter, "what if you make a mistake?"

"Simple," answered the artist. "I just tear down the wall."

The third of the remarkable triumvirate of mural painters who aroused the whole art world to the previously neglected area of mural work was David Alfaro Siqueiros, the only one who is still alive. He is still working, constantly producing easel work and murals.

Another stormy petrel, like Diego, he has been in and out of prison for various reasons and has always been a vociferous and tireless friend of every leftist cause. His work is as personal and distinguished as that of Diego Rivera or Orozco; his own forte is the ability to give sculptural roundness to his figures and enormous depth to his panoramas. Like the other two, he is capable of depicting rhythmic movement and speed and of organizing great crowds into acceptable and meaningful compositions.

Several other modern painters have made Mexico's name respected in Europe and in the Americas. The outstanding one among them is Rufino Tamayo, who has done some murals, but whose major work is on canvas. Born in Oaxaca, he found that there was little place in Mexico for one more aspiring painter, especially when his interest was in color and design and not in revolutionary themes. So, since no man is a prophet in his own country, he went to New York and to Paris, where he established a sound reputation as a great colorist and as a moving and sensitive artist. There are many who feel that he is the greatest of the living Mexican painters.

Juan O'Gorman, an architect by profession, is also an extremely able muralist and easel painter. He designed the outside murals for several Mexican buildings, outstanding among them the library of the National University of Mexico. His designs are carried out in mosaic, the small stones being used in their natural colors, so that no amount of sun or stormy weather can alter them.

A painter whose true name was Gerardo Murillo, born in Jalisco, took the name of Atl (meaning water), although his own passion was for mountains. He experimented with theories for showing space, and was interested in clouds and cloud effects. Many of his works are in museums.

Other outstanding Mexican painters, who have done some murals but whose reputations rest upon their easel painting, are Manuel Rodriguez Lozano, Federico Cantú (who has done many religious subjects), Guerrero Galván, whose work reflects the poetry and sensitivity of his Indian subjects, and several women, among them Frida Kahlo, whose work was largely introspective and even autobiographical, and of constant excellence, María Izquierdo, and others. Some foreign painters much identified with Mexico who have achieved critical and popular acclaim are Leonora Carrington, an Englishwoman, whose paintings reveal a rich fancy and excellent composition, and Remedios Varo, a Spaniard, whose work has become sought after by many museums, especially since her death while at the height of her powers. She was a remarkably fine painter, whose work shows domination of technique, much poetry, surface perfection, subtle color, and moving, though fantastic, subject matter.

Among the younger artists building up fame at the moment, one must mention José Luis Cuevas, whose work can be classified with that of Daumier and of Goya, being grotesque, mordant, and savage.

In the field of sculpture there are the classicists, like Armando Quesada and Fideas Elizondo, and a great number of younger artists working in the abstract and free fields, among whom should be mentioned Angela Gurria and Helen Escobedo, both young women still, who will have long careers ahead.

The Mexican spirit seems to express itself in plasticity, so it is natural that besides sculpture and painting, the Mexicans should excel in acting and in ballet.

Since the formation some ten years ago of the Ballet Folklórico of Mexico, under the guidance of Amalia Hernández, herself a dancer and an extraordinary choreographer, the great cities of the world have seen young Mexican dancers portraying many phases of Mexican life, from the beginning of its history to the present day, in authentic costumes, and with appropriate music.

No one who has watched performances of any one of the splendid companies touring the world as the Mexican Folkloric Ballet can forget the color, vivacity, and charm of the "Wedding in Jalisco," the languor and grace of the "Zandunga," embodying all the enchantment of the tropics, or the moving recollection of the courage and verve of the brave women who followed their men into the Revolution as "soldaderas."

It is not too much to say that the Mexican Folkloric Ballet has done for the country what Russian ballet did for Russia in the early years of this century. It has given the country of its origin a fame and an appreciation never gained through any other of the arts.

In the world of the theater Mexico is very active, and every city of any size in the Republic has a professional theater and several groups of enthusiastic amateurs. In Mexico City, often twelve to twenty small theaters are open at the same time, presenting many plays from the Broadway stage in translation, but also providing a proscenium for the works of many Mexican dramatists, among them Salvador Novo, Luis Basurto, Rodolfo Usigli, and others. In the world of the cinema, Luis Buñuel has won an enviably high position for originality and talent.

Mexico has seen a renaissance in literature in recent years. The breaking down of rigid forms in the novel, short story, and poetry has opened the way for a full display of the Mexican genius for satire, for fantastic exaggeration, for wit, and for imaginative use of the rich folklore, legend, history, and tradition of Mexico. To name a few: Martín Luis Guzmán, Juan Rulfo, Carlos Fuentes, Juan José Arreola, Luis Spota, Salvador Elizondo, and Rosario Castellanos.

Mariano Azuela began the great tradition of the "revolutionary novel" with his moving *Los de Abajo,* translated as *The Underdogs.*

Augustín Yañez, a writer of excellent novels, is best known for his remarkable study of a provincial town obsessed first with a smothering religious ritual and later with the revolution, *Al filo del Agua.*

After the great Sor Juana Inés de la Cruz, there were no poets of unusual quality in Mexico until late in the nineteenth and early in the twentieth century. Then there was a blossoming of rare and lovely lyric and romantic poetry, almost all of it with a strong Mexican inspiration. López Velarde, who sang nostalgically of his Mexican countryside and the innocent beauty of Mexican provincial señoritas, is not to be forgotten, nor Manuel Acuña, who killed himself because of unrequited love. Others were Díaz Mirón, Luis Urbina, and the internationally known Amado Nervo. In our day we have such masters of the poetic form as Jaime Torres Bodet, Salvador Novo, Javier Villaurrutia, and Carlos Pellicer.

Each of the modern novelists has a style remarkably original and incisive. Martín Luis Guzmán writes with profound knowledge of the Mexican Revolution. Juan Rulfo illumines the spirit and fantasies of the *mestizo* and the Indian, in small provincial villages. Rosario Castellanos portrays the fascinating Indian cultures of the south. Salvador Elizondo is certainly one of the most original writers, having invented several new techniques and forms.

One must not forget Bruno Traven, an American-born Scandinavian who made Mexico his home and wrote superbly of Mexico's people and problems in a series of excellent novels.

Mexico's musicians have also flowered in the early years of this century. Mexican music has traced an upward spiral —from the liturgical works of the time of the Conquest, which were based on the exquisitely subtle native music, through the flourishing of a genuinely Mexican folk song, to the development of composers in the symphonic style.

The work songs of the mounted vaqueros, and the use of the guitar for *serenatas* (that being one of the classical ways of wooing a maiden), gave rise to a kind of music that has been taken up and imitated by popular composers throughout the world. These songs are preserved and sung still, and are enormously popular in Mexico.

During the early years of the century, through the time of chaos and revolution and on into the present day, Mexico has spontaneously produced a kind of folk song known as the *corrido,* which recounts a story. This is usually a ballad, with romantic overtones, but always it deals with some violent or bloody event. A great many of these seem to fit political situations too, and they reflect the fatalistic, and yet critical, character of the Mexican.

In the field of learned, or composed, music, the leader in opening up the field was Manuel Ponce, many of whose simple songs are considered classics. He wrote a great deal of symphonic and concert music as well.

Following him, the genius of Silvestre Revueltas produced music of brilliant color, vitality, and energy.

Undoubtedly, the dominant figure in Mexican music for the last forty years has been Carlos Chávez, who besides composing a large body of work—symphonic, choral, operatic, and selections for piano and voice—has built up a national symphonic orchestra and prepared a group of young musicians in the art of conducting.

Carlos Chávez, a man of iron self-discipline and great energy, was determined to teach the Mexican public to appreciate all the worthwhile music of their century and of the past, for until he set himself to carry out this task, Mexicans dedicated themselves to Italian opera, to the piano music of Chopin and Beethoven, and to a limited sampling of the great symphonic works. He assailed reluctant Mexican ears with modernists like Stravinsky (they adored him, once they had recovered from the initial shock) and Schönberg (to his later works they remained cold), taught them to appreciate Brahms and Wagner, and carried out a patriotic and artistic duty in performing all worthy compositions by living composers, and by Mexicans in particular.

He also undertook the difficult matter of teaching Mexicans to be on time. "In Mexico, two things generally start on time," he said. "The bullfight, and mass. To those, now please add the concerts of the National Symphony Orchestra."

And they started on time, though often, it must be related sadly, to houses with only a few listeners. The full audience always seemed to arrive about half an hour late.

There are some things about which Mexicans will not allow themselves to be remodeled.

13

When you mention the Revolution in Mexico, you mean only one—the great land revolution, the complete upheaval and renewal that began in 1910. According to scholars, this revolution lasted until 1940, but many political leaders, sociologists, and students of history consider that it is still going on.

No doubt the Revolution was inevitable, even though the revolutionaries found specific reasons for its beginnings. Mexico, like the South before the Civil War, was living in an economy that was outmoded and bound to fail; a very few people were living on the labor of an enormous group of others, who were being deprived of their rights and of their liberty.

Life in the countryside was carried out in the main on

160

enormous haciendas worked by a crowd of simple laborers paid so little that they became literally enslaved, by their debts, to the hacienda stores, or to the *patrón*. The *patrón* himself was often living in Europe or traveling, leaving the administration of his lands to a *capataz*, a hired manager, who naturally tried, more than ever, to squeeze advantages of every kind from the laborers. Worse, great tracts of Mexico's land were held by foreigners, who took their profits out of the country and who demanded protection from their own embassies whenever there was any sign of rebellion or revolt among the workers on their lands.

In the cities, things were little better, from the point of view of simple justice. There was a great and growing bulk of people who had almost no money, and there was a wealthy aristocracy, which treated them with scorn, or at best with occasional worried charity. No solution to the troubles of the poor seemed to be in sight. Don Porfirio (President Díaz), who had entered office in 1877 as a popular military hero, had allowed himself to be re-elected and re-elected while his cronies and favorites dug themselves in, for life, in privileged positions.

Industry was in the hands of foreigners who operated the mines, the streetcars, the railways, the oil wells, and manufacturing, shipping their profits out to Canada, to the United States, to England, to Germany, to France. Mexicans were used only for the most unskilled labor, and when they demanded unions, or tried to strike, they were put down as ruthlessly as were the rebelling Indian tribes to the north.

In fact, the Yaqui uprisings against the government resulted in the hated *leva*, which was a kind of impressment into the army. Squads of military men roamed the streets of the cities after dark and literally kidnapped men who were out, carrying them off to the army. As would be assumed, it was the poor and defenseless who were picked up, not rich men, who could purchase their freedom from the *leva* with a handful of pesos.

All these difficulties, troubles, and abuses (not all of them the acts of selfish men, but many of them the natural consequences of many years of neglect of the changing social order) boiled up into general unrest. It is a truism that when people feel, rightly or wrongly, that they have nothing to lose, they will break out into revolution. This happened in Mexico in 1910.

The first revolutionists clustered around a man named Francisco Madero. He was the son of a rich family in northern Mexico, a person who had been brought up with every privilege and luxury. He was an idealist—gentle, kindly, genuinely unselfish and disinterested—who saw the abuses and wanted to change them. Madero had a great admiration for democratic processes and trusted in them. He himself did not want violence, war, fighting, and death. When pushed into action, he kept the fighting at a minimum and at the first opportunity arranged that Mexico should hold a free election. He was elected president, and great things were expected of him. But the forces of privilege and power and envy were stronger than Madero and his followers. He had not been in office many months before he was assassinated, and with him the duly elected vice-president, Pino Suárez.

It is now generally known that the man who planned and ordered the murders was Victoriano Huerta, a military

The Basilica of Our Lady of Guadalupe

*A portion of a fresco by Diego Rivera which hangs in the
National Palace in Mexico City*

Peace *by José Clemente Orozco, at the National Preparatory College*

Self-Portrait *by David Alfaro Siqueiros shown during an exhibit at the Museum of Modern Art, Mexico City*

Skilled hands make beautiful and useful objects from clay

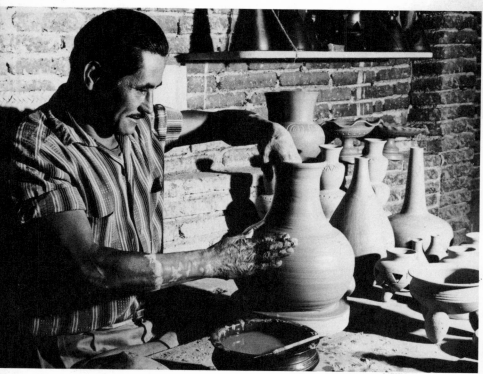

*The Ballet Folklorico performs the Dance of the Quetzales
(Quetzal birds)*

Central Library, University of Mexico, is decorated with a mural by Juan O'Gorman. It represents the Spanish colonial period of Mexican history

Pancho Villa in action during the revolution

*Children often served as messengers,
sentries, or even soldiers*

Villa's followers lived crudely, eating whatever they could whenever they could. Women and children were an integral part of most revolutionary camps

leader who wanted power for himself. But there was a simple man in the north who had believed in Madero and had loved him. His true name was Doroteo Arango, but he had killed a man to avenge his sister's honor when he was still a young boy, and he had been a fugitive and a bandit in the years since, having taken the name of Francisco or "Pancho" Villa. Pancho Villa had suffered at the hands of the rich *hacendados,* and he had followed "little Mr. Madero" in the hope that his reforms would mean a change for the poor and miserable people of Mexico. When Madero was assassinated, Villa rose up in arms, and a true revolution began—a war of desperate men against authority, of men who felt they had nothing to lose and everything to gain.

Villa was a man of great magnetism, despite his ignorance, and he was a born leader. Military experts who have studied his campaigns report that he was a remarkable strategist. It is said that the brilliant German General Rommel, known as the "Desert Fox" to the British, carefully studied all Villa's campaigns, for their extraordinary skill in guerrilla warfare. It is believed that Villa invented (and certainly used with great success) the "pincer" movement of troops.

In the south there rose up another hero who like Villa was a man of the earth, poor and disinherited, who really represented the forgotten people of Mexico. He was Emiliano Zapata. Born and brought up in the state of Morelos, a section of many rich haciendas, he had seen the encroachments of the large landholders upon the lands held by poor native farmers; he had seen the "little man" forced out time after time, and left without any land to work. Looking around, he observed that, in general, land was not owned by the very men who worked it.

Zapata also rose up in arms, and he soon had a large following. His battle cry was "Land for the man who works it!" Throughout all the years of violence and trouble, whenever he was called to a conference table or otherwise approached by one faction or another, he held stubbornly to his demand that there must be land reform, that land must not be held by foreigners or by rich patrons who lived in the city and in Europe, but must be given out to the men who labor on it.

At first hopeful and reasonable, Zapata tried to keep his followers under control and to await redress of the wrongs to the country men. His men wore little pictures of the Virgin of Guadalupe sewed to their hats. But as years went by, and one faction fought another in a continual effort to seize power—as treachery followed treachery and assassination followed assassination—he lost patience, and he began to attack and set fire to the haciendas of the south. Zapata became feared and hated, as Villa was feared and hated, by the rich, the foreigners, and the large landowners of the north and central Mexico.

Neither man had any backing in the way of money with which to buy arms and horses, so both resorted to seizing cattle and grain to feed their men, horses for them to ride, and whatever gold or money they could take, in an attack on a town or a ranch, to be used for the purchase of arms.

The role played by the United States during the turmoil was not always admirable, though it followed the usual procedure of any foreign nation that tries to protect its own

164

nationals and their property during an uprising. Efforts were made to bring the warring factions to peace, but in the meantime, merchants from the United States traveled in Mexico and sold arms and ammunition to either side, and to both.

Villa, who was perspicacious, soon realized that the man who held the few railway lines into Mexico held the balance of power, for he could move troops, arms, and food. Villa's campaigns therefore centered around the towns that were railway centers.

There were many revolutionary leaders who rose up in arms and either campaigned by themselves or went to join one or another of the revolutionary generals. On many occasions a leader would arouse a town, the men would line up, armed with their rifles, and simply march away to war. As they fell into line, usually a crowd of women would follow, carrying cooking pots, what little food they had on hand, and sometimes small babies, slung into their rebozos and tied on their backs. As we have seen, these women (known as *soldaderas*) were a phenomenon of the Mexican Revolution, one that has not occurred in any other uprising.

The Revolution dragged on. After Huerta another leader rose in the north. A former schoolmaster, Venustiano Carranza had been governor of the state of Coahuila. He called a meeting of governors and proposed a constitutional congress, for his rallying cry was that the convulsed country should have a constitution to live by, so that rules could be obeyed, elections held, and peace achieved.

Villa did not trust him; neither did Zapata, for Carranza made only perfunctory promises about giving land to the men who worked it. Battles and more unrest ensued. A young leader in the northwest, Álvaro Obregón, then joined his forces to Carranza's. Being a man of some military genius, he began to win battles. When he defeated Villa, it seemed that the Revolution might be over. Yet Carranza also was assassinated, and after some elections had been held and Obregón took office, he too was assassinated.

Yet the Revolution had accomplished what it set out to do, even though the leaders had gone down, one after the other, before the bullets of assassins. Zapata was ambushed by treachery and shot down. So was Villa. Many others, of less fame, met the same fate.

The reports in the American press of these numerous murders led many Americans to think of the Mexican Revolution as nothing but chaos and turmoil. Yet the main objects that had been fought for were accomplished. A sweeping land reform was begun, and it is still going on today. Land is being assigned, in *parcelas*, or subsistence farms, to independent poor farmers. In sections where land had been worked communally in times gone by, a system of giving out the lands to a community, rather than to single individuals, was tried; in many instances this has worked very well. This is known as the *ejido* system, and a great many villagers find it answers their needs, as they are used to village life and like to live in a community, the men going out to work the communal lands daily.

The resented "succession" of Porfirio Díaz to the presidency, term after term, has been taken care of by a provision in the new constitution, which says, "No re-election."

To this day, as a kind of theme, all government announcements and documents bear this statement, "No re-election, and effective suffrage."

The new constitution, which was drafted in 1917 and by which Mexico is governed, is one of the most liberal to be found anywhere. It sets forth strong protection for labor, outlines land reform, and accords universal suffrage. Despite the constitution, however, it was actually only recently that women were given the vote in certain states, and in some others they still do not exercise it fully.

Some articles of the constitution are fought regularly, especially the one dealing with education, which specifically prohibits any sort of religious instruction. Many parents feel that this is an infringement of their rights to freedom of worship. So far, no one has been able to achieve any change in the strict provisions of Article Three, dealing with education.

Definitely part of the Revolution, and growing out of it, was the expropriation of any oil companies that, after due and repeated warnings, refused to comply with the terms by which they had been given permission to operate in Mexico. These terms provided that, aside from necessary technical officers, the main administration of the work should be performed by Mexicans, and that the oil companies should cease to arm and equip and use their own police forces. Companies that complied with these (and other) requirements were not affected, but when many of the great oil companies defied the Mexican government and proposed to continue business more or less as small independent powers within the borders of Mexico, President

Lázaro Cárdenas, an old revolutionary himself, used his powers, under the constitution, to expropriate them.

Under Mexican law (and this is true of other Latin American countries), all resources below the surface of the earth belong to the government and may not be claimed by any individual or company. They may be leased by the government for exploitation, under certain conditions, but they may revert to the government at any time.

The Revolution still goes on, for the strongest political party is the one that calls itself the Party of Revolutionary Institutions. This is obligated to continue to carry out the reforms that were fought for in the Revolution.

Land reform continues, and a large section of the budget is set aside for education. Though presidents may not be re-elected, most of the politicians active and powerful in the PRI (Party of Revolutionary Institutions) are now over sixty, and there is a restless discontent among younger men, who feel that the party itself has been in power too long and has taken too much trouble to keep its "strong men" in power. Other parties have been formed, and one or two have been able to send representatives to the House of Deputies.

As one looks at the social structure of Mexico, it becomes obvious that the Revolution gained most of its goals. The people are being educated; a middle class is rising; labor is strong and well protected. The one sector of the public that has not benefited as much as the others is the *campesino*, or country worker. Despite land reform, disenchanted country workers continue to stream into the cities, where they find no work, and gradually settle into a life of poverty, idleness, and despair.

Attempts are being made to solve this problem, which will be greatly alleviated when all the great dams being constructed are actually put into service. Then much more land will be available for cultivation, and probably many country workers will return to their farms and ranches.

14

It may come as a surprise to many people who think of Mexico as a "revolutionary country," and who remember the Revolution as a time of violence, chaos, murder, and starvation, that Mexico has contributed to the world many remarkable legal attitudes and political postures of nobility and justice.

During the early years of the Colony when the Inquisition was established, there were no prisons in which to hold the persons judged to be deliberately acting against the state and the state religion, which was Catholicism. Since the Inquisition wished whenever possible to bring people back into the Church, it often did not recommend a civil trial, but instead put the defendant in the charge of a priest, under promise to study with the priest, or "under parole." There is some reason to think that the principle of parole, which passed over into our own penal systems, originated in this way. At the same time it is interesting to note in passing that while people were "on parole" they were sentenced to work in hospitals for wounded Spanish soldiers. Thus, the Inquisition in Mexico was instrumental in working out a system of redeeming prisoners by re-education.

Another Mexican legal procedure that is unique in the world is called *amparo*—a Spanish word meaning protection, shelter, or refuge. The name is used for a document, which any citizen may demand of the court, to protect him against any other legal act by authorities that might deprive him of his life, his property, or his liberty.

In American law (based on English common law), the only protections the citizen has against the state, in legal procedures, are the habeas corpus and the warrant. He may not be brought before any court of law without a writ to demand his presence, nor may his property be searched without a warrant. But in Mexico, if a man suspects that he may be brought to court for any reason—real or trumped up—he may provide himself with an *amparo*. Meanwhile, he can instigate investigations, to learn the nature of the charge against himself, and he has time to prepare his defense.

Another interesting provision of Mexican law deals with the charge of murder, or homicide. There are degrees of homicide (and punishment is meted out according to the degree), but in order for a homicide to be considered "in the first degree," it must fulfill the following conditions: premeditation, personal advantage, surprise—and yet one other, which is "betrayal of trust." Thus, if a man murders his wife, or his brother, or a friend, or any other person who trusted him, his crime is worse.

In Mexico, only a few states carry out capital punishment, and that rarely. There is a way in which police officers evade the law, however, and often it is done in the case of hardened criminals who have committed very terrible crimes. This is called *la ley fuga*, which means the "law of the escape." If a criminal is being transferred from one jail to another and tries to escape, the officers in charge may try to stop him by shooting at him and even killing him.

In general, Mexican laws are humane and sensible. A man may be sentenced to twenty years in prison for a crime of passion, the feeling being that the particular circumstances that brought him to commit the crime probably will not be duplicated in just the same way, and therefore he is not likely to offend once more.

Mexican penal institutions permit the "marital visit," for married criminals, and even allow the common-law wife to visit, if the couple has lived openly together for some time. This law avoids much trouble, fighting, and rage among the prisoners. The visits of their wives keep up their hope, bring them news of family, and comfort them.

It is also a Mexican law (now followed by some other countries) that no child may be considered illegitimate. Any child who has been recognized by the father may inherit, share and share alike with legitimate children, upon the father's death. This is perhaps hard on legitimate wives, who may resent the fact that their own children have to share an estate with the children of any adventure or "in-

172

discretion." But the Mexican law quite rightly sees only that innocent children should not have to pay in any way for the character defects of their parents.

In the fields of international law and of diplomacy, Mexico has an enviable record. She has never carried out a war to annex land and has never taken part in any war to secure economic or other advantage. Her wars have been one hundred percent defensive.

Even in the matter of the Alamo, which is taught in American schools as the massacre of a handful of brave men by a relentless and cruel army, it is well to review the facts. When a number of Americans petitioned Mexico for the right to settle in Mexican territory (the land that is now Texas), the right was granted, provided the settlers observed Mexican law and promised to safeguard Mexican rights. Yet the land was coveted for settlement, in the hope it could be made into another slave state and restore the balance of slave-state power to the South. Of course, many settlers had no wish or plan to own slaves, but others did. The settlers, once they were numerous, wanted to get free from Mexico and join the United States, and they started a rebellion with this in mind. No doubt they had many excellent reasons for wishing to join their own countrymen. The fact is they broke their promise to respect Mexican law, and Santa Anna was sent to put down the rebellion. This he did, with great cruelty, as everyone knows. Yet, legally, Mexico had plenty of justification for taking the military action she did, and it must be remembered that the men holding the Alamo refused to surrender.

In all her foreign diplomatic relations, Mexico stands fast with the principle of "self-determination of peoples."

She is adamant against the forceful imposing of the will of one nation on another.

Believing that the Cuban revolution was a true revolution of the people, carried out without foreign troops (supplies and moral support are something no one can assess completely), Mexico has not refused to trade or deal with Castro's Cuba. On the other hand, Mexico has stubbornly continued to refuse to recognize Franco's Spain, even though both contenders in the Spanish Civil War had help and troops from foreign countries on their soil—Franco from Germany and Italy, and the Republicans from Russia and from other countries that sent Communist-sympathetic brigades.

Thus, many Mexicans do not approve the intervention of American troops in Vietnam, for their national ideal is non-intervention in the internal quarrels of any other country.

It must be remembered, of course, that Mexico is not a first-rate power and does not reason that she must support or hold a line of defense anywhere. None of Mexico's borders is fortified.

In every international conference to propose peace measures, Mexico is active and hopeful. She is among the sponsors of programs to outlaw atomic power for war. During the Olympic Games, Mexico continuously carried out a theme of International Peace, being the first host-country for the games that had ever done so.

15

Modern Mexico faces a host of problems, but thanks to her geographical position and to her firm attitude, which forbids any official meddling in the internal affairs of other nations, her problems are not those of defense.

Mexico's problems are social.

A very large proportion of the people are still in need of education, of gainful employment, of some access to the manufactured goods being produced in their native country. There is a heavy migration of unhappy and poverty-sticken country people into the cities, where they are not absorbed by industry and where they live miserable lives. There are still villages that have not really been integrated into the greater Mexico, villages where the people do not speak Spanish or understand any of the possibilities for advancement now available.

Add to this need for social help of several kinds the fact that an extremely high birth rate complicates the problems and makes it difficult for the government to catch up. Ten years ago the population of Mexico was 33 million. Today it passes 50 million.

What is being done?

First, there are a number of organizations that devote themselves exclusively to trying to better the lot of the predominantly Indian villages. The government operates a Department of Indian Affairs, which sends out trained teams to teach the villagers Spanish, the elements of hygiene, better farming methods, ways of growing new foods that will benefit their general health, and methods of building adequate homes and providing themselves with potable water.

Much credit must be given, also, to the various religious missions to the Indians of many districts: the Jesuits in the mountains where the Tarahumaras live; the Maryknoll Fathers in Yucatán; the CENAMI, a Catholic organization which sends out field workers to live with and help Indian villagers in any part of the country, and which has translated the Bible into many Indian tongues; and a number of Protestant missions, which have done valuable educational and health work in many parts of the country.

And one must not forget the enthusiastic college and high-school workers from many sections of the United States who come willingly to work to help the most desperately needy.

In a poor village south of Cuernavaca, for instance, lives a young black American who had been extremely unhappy in the United States, bitter about the troubles of his race, and in general feeling hopeless. Visiting Mexico, he became interested in teaching youngsters how to play baseball. Now he has made his home in one of the villages, has teams started in many nearby *pueblos*, and is conducting playoffs. At the same time, he teaches the children English and otherwise makes himself useful to the whole village. He is much appreciated, the town provides him with a room and food, and he himself says that he never before knew what happiness was.

The lot of the worker in the cities is steadily improving, thanks to industrial development, the organization of labor unions, and the attitude of the country and the courts, which generally favor labor in a dispute.

Anyone who has been employed for more than three months may not be dismissed from his job for any reason except chronic alcoholism or absenteeism. Once he has been kept on for more than three months, it is assured that he has proven competence to the satisfaction of the employer. If he is dismissed after that time, he must be paid three months' salary, plus a month's salary for every year he has worked.

If a strike is called against any factory or business, a board of mediators, appointed by industry, labor, and the government, must meet to decide whether the strike is legitimate (legal). If the strike is declared illegal, workers must return to work at once. If it is legal, there must be adjustments. If an employer has been adjudged recalcitrant about ameliorating grievances that have caused a legal strike, he is liable to expropriation; that is, the government may seize the business or factory and turn it over to the workers.

The workers are also helped by the social-security system, by which a worker pays out a percentage of his income, which amount is then duplicated by his employer and by the government, the whole being held for him until retirement. However, he may, in case of need, borrow against it, at a low interest. Some workers are not yet protected by social security, among them domestic servants and farm workers. However, both these groups will be incorporated into the system before long.

At present, domestic employees are protected by law to this degree: if they are injured or become ill while in the service of a householder, the employer is liable for their medical expenses and may not discharge them without paying them the full three months' salary, plus the bonus of a month's salary for each year of employment.

In the field of education, Mexico is making remarkable strides forward. Schools are being built apace, and many private groups are building schools as well, to aid the government in this tremendous task. Teachers are encouraged to work in rural districts, and many of them seek this sort of difficult work out of patriotism.

The government now publishes and distributes, free, textbooks to be used in the first six grades, which are compulsory throughout Mexico. After the sixth grade, the child enters secondary school or high school.

One of the most important developments in education has been the plan to augment federal help to all provincial universities, so that they may give degrees in all the professions, as well as in the humanities. This would not only be of great interest to professors, for it would open up new teaching posts, but would greatly decongest the National University in Mexico City.

In the field of health, Mexico has made tremendous strides which are wholly admirable. Health brigades sent out to exterminate the anopheles mosquito (carrier of malaria) have almost totally cleaned up breeding places for this insect. One may see everywhere in provincial towns, painted on house, wall, and hut, the sign indicating that the place has been disinfected of mosquitoes. And indeed, practically the only cases of malaria now known are those that predate the current campaign.

In cleaning out malaria, the authorities have controlled a great deal of tuberculosis in the country, too, for tuberculosis easily develops in an organism weakened by many bouts of malarial fever. Other health problems are being attacked, largely by means of roving ambulances equipped to inoculate the people in remote districts (smallpox is now almost unknown in Mexico) and by means of clinics and hospitals in larger towns.

The high rate of infant mortality has been Mexico's most serious health problem. Now the health of children is protected from the earliest age. All babies must be vaccinated against smallpox and infantile paralysis. Brigades travel the country continuously, taking care of this and checking against any diseases that might affect the eyes. Every school child is given the patch test for tuberculosis, and the vaccine against the illness is administered by social-security clinics.

The health problem to which the government is now giving the most concentrated attention is intestinal disorders. These may be attributed primarily to water and water-born diseases. First, the government, through its Department of Hydraulic Resources, is gradually and steadily seeing to it that every center of population in the country has potable water. Second, markets are being cleaned up in all cities of any size, and soon inspection of country markets will begin. Tourists who deplore the new modern markets, with running water and concrete floors that can be hosed off at night, should remember that clean markets would solve most of the digestive problems they complain of.

As it is, many visitors to Mexico who do not do what most Mexicans do—that is, drink only purified water and eat only cooked vegetables, and fruits that may be washed and peeled—become ill for a few days. Part of this fear of Mexican food is hysterical in origin. Mexicans visiting the United States often fall ill, too, because they are unaccustomed to the chemicals in the water and to the foods. Reasonable precautions are in order in all tropical countries.

During the Olympic Games, all athletes ate at the same tables, and among many hundreds of athletes there were only two cases of intestinal disorder. The training tables all supplied Mexican milk, butter, and fruits in abundance. The Russian athletes, when asked if they followed any special diet, replied that they did. They were allowed to eat everything they wanted, with the exception of foods made with wheat flour. (This was a precaution against gaining weight.)

Dr. José González Gutíerrez, a young doctor who was for some years in service at one of the large hotels in Mexico City, who has often been called in to treat intestinal disorders among tourists, said: "Tourists who come here are in the first place wrought up and nervous because of getting ready for their vacation, catching a plane, and flying to a city very much higher than the average city in the United States or Europe. The increased altitude slows down digestion, and the general nervous state of the visitor makes him vulnerable. Even those who drive here arrive tired out, and perhaps they have not taken reasonable care along the road. Then, once here, since they are on vacation, visitors tend to eat too heavily and to drink too much. The Mexican rule of a large meal at midday, with a rest afterward to aid digestion, and a very light supper, not taken too late, is almost never followed by visitors. They tend to take several drinks before a late dinner, diluting their digestive juices, and then they eat what they like in the United States—meals of meat and salad. It is no surprise that most of them have to endure a more or less severe digestive disturbance. Due to much adverse propaganda, the moment they feel intestinal twinges, they become very excited and fearful, and this makes them worse."

Probably the most pressing and severe of Mexico's problems is one shared by every country on the globe, the United States not excepted. This is the attempt to bring up the general purchasing power, the level of comfort and of well-being, of the great numbers of people in the country who are at poverty level. And poverty level in Mexico, in the countryside, means far less than is considered poverty level in affluent United States. There are many families who exist on a very little beyond what is actually needed to sustain life. They must first be given gainful employment, next housing, then purchasing power.

As reported, the government, for all its efforts, is always behind on this problem because of the high birth rate and the steadily decreasing rate of mortality. People live longer, their children do not die as they did previously, and more babies are born and survive.

There is criticism and unrest because there is no doubt that while a heavy underlying layer of the population is in dire need, a small percentage of the population has extraordinary wealth—and many of these display that wealth callously. A further cause of discontent, especially among the young, is the fact that older men in government and in the professions are loath to step down or to release their power in any way. This, however, seems to be a difficulty throughout the whole world and, again, seems to be linked to the population explosion, for more and more young men are coming into their best productive years and are avid for a chance to work and prove themselves. What seems likely to happen in Mexico, as elsewhere, is that suddenly a whole new wave of young people, having a new outlook, will move into government and business and will probably make sweeping changes in the whole pattern of life in the country.

Despite criticisms, despite pressing problems, Mexico has gone forward in many ways that are obvious at a glance.

Lic. Gustavo Díaz Ordaz, the president, is the fourth consecutive Mexican president who is a civilian. In other words, the threat of military dictatorship, so much feared in Latin American countries, seems far in the past. Furthermore, the top positions in government are occupied, with more and more frequency, by men who are not so much professional politicians as technicians, and this cannot but bring the country into the forward-forging group of modern nations. An engineer is head of the Department of

Communications; a skilled economist is head of the Treasury; a brilliant career diplomat is chief of the Department of Foreign Relations—and so on through most of the great positions of importance and all the others which depend on them. The men guiding Mexico today are men who have been well trained in the special fields they undertake to administer.

Mexico is well on a fair and clear road toward development, progress, and prosperity.

16

And after one has studied Mexican geography, history, sociology, traditions, what remains? After one has traveled from the north to the south, has flown over the mountains and lakes and rivers, and has explored the cities, what stays in the mind and memory?

Color.

One remembers the tan and soft cream of desert stretches, the mountains purpling at dusk, the spectacular sunsets. One sees the deep sapphire blue of the seas, changing to jade green and cream at the edges, where the waves break on the long white beaches. One recalls the buildings of dark red *tezontli* in Mexico City, the pale green stone of the constructions in Oaxaca, the dazzling "white city" which is Mérida.

Perhaps what remains in the memory is the look of the streets and sidewalks in Cuernavaca and Tehuacán, Puebla, and Mexico City in jacaranda time, when the very air seems to have turned purple from the quantity of blossoms. Or maybe one remembers the silver and green of Xochimilco—tall green poplars and the silvery surface sheen of all the canals and streams. Or the rich jungle-green of the vegetation in the southern states. Or the warm brown of the skin of the country people, dressed in white, walking beside their little dun-colored burros, with wagging ears and dainty hoofs, the cross marked plainly on each little donkey's back, under his burden.

Sounds.

The cathedral and church bells—whether you are hearing the bass-booming and deep-tongued bells of Mexico City's cathedral and "old town" churches, or the insistent clanging of village church bells, they give unforgettable sound to living, which we have almost forgotten in our American cities.

Add to this the baying of dogs at the moon; you will hear this sound in every small town in Mexico, and people who have left Mexico to live in other places miss it very much. The Spanish poet, García Lorca, phrased it "a horizon of dogs, barking very far away . . ."

And the serenades! Saint's days still summon forth the musicians, with guitars, trumpets, and a singer, who bring dawn serenades to Lolas on their day, to the Carmens, to the Marías (on the fifteenth of August), to Conchas on December 8, and so on and so on. This custom persists even in Mexico City, with its eight million inhabitants, and makes the evenings and the dawns lovely with melody. In many towns, too, guitar players swing up onto the buses and strum and sing for a few blocks, then pass the hat to collect a few centavos. It relieves the wearisome daily ride through traffic.

Fragrances.

The pines and cedars along all the mountain highways. The gardenias of Fortín, where the waxy-white flowers grow in such quantities that they are tossed into the swimming pools, to make the daily dip an exotic pleasure. The unforgettable acrid, tantalizing odor of toasted chili-peppers, being prepared out-of-doors for some street-corner *puesto* of Mexican tidbits. The strange, haunting smell of charcoal smoke, in Mexican villages. The fragrance of fine perfume, cut velvet of armchairs, and drifting cigarette smoke from the lobby of the great theater of Bellas Artes, during opera season. The overpowering scents—spicy, ferny, and blossom-sweet—of the flower markets.

Impressions that one carries away from Mexico—little flashing images that one never forgets, and that mean Mexico forever:

The two pacing horses in Chapultepec Park, with two riders impeccably dressed in *charro* costume, velvet trousers, laced with silver, and sweeping-brimmed sombreros— one a man, erect and easy in the saddle, the other his small son of four, equally erect and proud.

The beam of the lighthouse from La Roqueta, sweeping over Acapulco Bay on a deeply black, moonless night, revealing in sudden brilliance the little boats rocking on the bay, the houses climbing up the hills, the expanse of heaving black water.

The beauty of a Guadalajara *señorita*, dressed in black,

186

her black lace mantilla framing a camellia-pale face, emerging from church on a Sunday morning.

The delicacy of the "butterfly nets" of the Janitzio fishermen, seen on an opalescent dawn, as they shove off from shore.

The gesture of an old woman in ruffled calico clothes, in the market, who solemnly makes the sign of the cross over her first sale of the day. (The money will be given to her favorite saint, imploring constant protection.)

Perhaps the vision that may remain is of a man, or a woman, with a sleeping child hung across his shoulder. This is seen everywhere, as Mexicans are family people and take their children with them on all excursions.

Or just a Mexican baby's face—silken black hair, enormous velvety dark eyes, apricot skin.

Or a trim, keen-eyed Mexican pilot, striding out to the plane he will guide through the skies as he takes the visitor home.

Or the colorful weaving figures of the National Folkloric Ballet in one of their exotic dances.

All mean Mexico. And each by itself can only hint at the variety, the profoundly tragic and violent past, the shining and hopeful future of Mexico and her people.

1858–1872	Benito Juárez
1872–1876	Lerdo de Tejada
1876	Porfirio Díaz
1876–1877	Juan M. Mendez
1877–1880	Porfirio Díaz
1880–1884	Manuel González
1884–1911	Porfirio Díaz
1911	F. León de la Barra
1911–1913	Francisco Indalecio Madero
1913	Pedro Lascurain
1913–1914	Victoriano Huerta
1914	F. Carvajal, and Venustiano Carranza
1914–1915	Eulalio Gutíerrez
1915	González Garza and Lagos Chazaro
1915–1920	Venustiano Carranza
1920–1924	Álvaro Obregón
1924–1928	Plutarco Elías Calles
1928–1930	Emilio Portes Gil
1930–1932	Pascual Órtiz Rubio
1932–1934	Abelardo Rodríguez
1934–1940	Lázaro Cárdenas
1940–1946	M. Ávila Camacho
1946–1952	Miguel Alemán
1952–1958	Adolfo Ruiz Cortines
1958–1964	Adolfo López Mateos
1964–1970	Gustavo Díaz Ordaz

c. 1325   Founding of Tenochtitlán (Mexico City)

1492   Columbus discovers America

1519   Hernán Cortes lands and marches up to Mexico City

1521   Mexico City conquered

1524   Arrival of first friars (12 Franciscans), whose task was to pacify and teach and convert the Indians
Council of the Indies formed to govern New Spain; viceregal period begins

1531   Appearances of Our Lady of Guadalupe to Juan Diego, a poor Indian

1810   First attempts to get freedom from Spain; Padre Hidalgo utters "Grito de Independencia"

1821   Mexico wins independence from Spain

1823   Mexico proclaimed Republic

1824   Federal Constitution proclaimed

1836   Rebellion of Texas

1845   Annexation of Texas to United States

1846   California and New Mexico taken by United States

1848   End of war with United States

1859   Benito Juárez proclaims reform laws, limiting power of Church

1864   French forces put Maximilian on throne of Mexico

1867   Maximilian surrenders; end of French Empire in Mexico

1876   Porfirio Díaz enters Mexico with revolutionary army and is proclaimed president

1910   Outbreak of Revolution. Leaders arise: Madero, Villa, Zapata, Carranza, Álvaro Obregón

1917   New constitution adopted in Mexico

1938   Mexico expropriates oil properties

1960   Mexico takes over electrical power for government control

Index